Sermon on the Mount by Jesus

Jesus Gnosis series, volume 1

Thomas Ragland

The Jesus Gnosis series is an interfaith collection of related scripture quotes to be used as a contemplative guide. The Sermon on the Mount by Jesus is focused upon a selection from the Christian text called the Gospel of Matthew.

Library of Congress Control Number: 2013906247

ISBN 978-0-9892511-0-5

Title: Sermon on the Mount by Jesus
Subtitle: Jesus Gnosis series, volume 1
Edition: 1
Publisher: Thomas Ragland
U.S. City: Nashville, TN
Author: Thomas Ragland
Editor: Thomas Ragland
Printing and Distribution Services: Lulu.com

Table of Contents

Jesus Gnosis series, volume 1

This study of the Sermon on the Mount, chapters 5 through 7 of the Gospel of Matthew, is intended to be the initial volume in a series of explorations in contemplation of the teachings and events associated with the Jesus that is the central focal point for the formation of Christianity.

"Jesus" is the English transliteration of the Greek name Iesous. This name was used by the Greeks to transliterate the Hebrew name that is "Joshua" in English. To the early Greek speaking Christians, Jesus and Joshua would have read as the exact same name. The name means salvation, which became a "key word hoped for promise" in Jewish literature. Along with Moses and Elijah, Jesus / Joshua was the only person legended to have climbed a mountain and encountered God face-to-face. This Jesus / Joshua led the chosen people across the river to their promised land. The New Testament Jesus is presented as teaching from a mountain with the authority of God, leading people to repent, come to the river and be baptized into a new life in pursuit of a kingdom not of this world. The diversity of views on the nature of Jesus will take volumes to explore. While advanced Christological discussions may accompany the studies of later Christian texts, we here stand at a very simple early snapshot of thoughts condensed and presented as what the perfect Teacher has to proclaim to his initiates from the vantage point of the mountain setting.

The word "Gnosis" is a bow to the early Christian Gnostics, in a romanticized form, imagined to primarily desire learning about God and about themselves through self-induced direct experiences of change and transformation. As such it stands up to "Pistis" which is more of the "having faith" side of things. Not that "faith in Wisdom", Pistis Sophia, is a bad thing, just that Gnosis brings the implications that the ideas were put into practice, the light was lit, the foundation built, the religious ideas evident in a transformed life and set of values and ambitions. As such an idealized imposed meaning of the word "Gnosis" is in play here, I cannot say with any certainly that this is how any of the ancient early Christians thought, it is just that in my vision that is how they should have approached Jesus.

One goal of the series is to place Jesus back within the contexts of a world of religious traditions that resonate in specific ideals and understandings of why defining values and visions and identifications is such an important task for the successful human experience of both the metaphysical and the mundane daily life. There has become a

Fundamentalist "Jesus out of context" that sees Jesus as so defendably unique in a world otherwise obscured. Early Christians would have had the context in mind, a context of a cosmopolitan fabric of a mixture of Western thoughts and Eastern influences, Jewish, Greek, Egyptian, in the near focus, but with the waves from the Far East not having been completely ignored.

In the case of the Sermon on the Mount, these external lights only prove to illuminate the concentrated Wisdom presented in this brief collection of values and ideals. Jesus takes the best of human thought, weaves it into a strong fabric and serves it back to us as a plan for Gnosis to transform our understanding of God, of ourselves, of culture, of principles, and of our ability and responsibility to change both ourselves and the world around us for the better.

What may subsequent volumes in this series prove? I can only hope that I can remain the vehicle through which this work is accomplished, and failing that, that this task is carried on in the wake I leave behind.

Thomas Ragland 2013

Influences

It is time to remove the text of the Sermon on the Mount from its hermetically sealed jar, and place it within its rightful context.

Jewish

The central scripture texts for the Jewish faith are the first five "books" of the Bible: Genesis, Exodus, Leviticus, Numbers, and Deuteronomy. Each of these are represented here. Genesis, to point out Abraham's blessing from God, his personal encounter, his quest for perfection in the sight of God. Exodus collects the directives from this "God encountered", has Moses climbing Mount Sinai to speak to God face-to-face. Leviticus continues with the quest to know what to do and how to live to achieve perfection in the sight of God. Numbers mentions salt being used to purify, a theme picked up on in the Sermon on the Mount. Deuteronomy presents more practical instructions for human relations and what it means to be a people of God.

In my mind, the Sermon on the Mount is divided into sections according to how it uses Jewish scripture for a framework: Abraham for blessing, Moses for laws, and the Prophets for dreams. It could be thought of as an encapsulation of, a summary of, a study guide for, the ancient Law, the Jewish ToWRaH. ToWRaH is a Hebrew word that could be thought of as a combination of two other Hebrew words, ToWB (good) and RaH (evil). It is this knowledge of good (thou shalts) and evil (thou shalt nots) that was thought to be key to making humanity right with God. Beyond even the famous "ten" commandments, Jews recognized 613 commandments present in the ToWRaH. How Jesus reacts to Law within the Sermon on the Mount is interesting. He doesn't run from Law, as could be interpreted from reading other Christian texts, but he seems to see it somewhat transcended by a truly heart-held living Gnosis. What does "thou shalt not kill" mean to someone who vows never to hate or take revenge in any way? What does "thou shalt not steal" mean to a monk with a vow of poverty?

Jewish scriptures and writings referenced here go beyond the ToWRaH to the Prophets. The Prophet texts included here are: Judges, Samuel, Kings, Amos, Ezekiel, Habakkuk, Isaiah, Jeremiah, and Zephaniah. Also included are the Writings: Chronicles, Daniel, Job, Lamentations, Proverbs, and Psalms. Thus far, we remain in familiar territory for the Christian carrying a Bible, for all of these are included in the same book as the Sermon on the Mount.

The Jews of the time of the Sermon on the Mount would not have been limited to the texts included in modern Bibles. The Greek Septuagint LXX version of the Jewish scriptures included additional texts. Two of these texts present ideas that are more at home with the teachings of Jesus in the Sermon on the Mount: Tobit (in Catholic Bibles) and Sirach (in Catholic Bibles). The few quotes from the Talmud are of interest, but it is The Dead Sea Scrolls that have given us insight into texts important at that time that have been forgotten: Jubilees, 1 Enoch, along with sectarian texts that present a backdrop for the context of the Sermon on the Mount: Community Rule, Damascus Document, and War Scroll. Pseudepigrapha supplies us with even more texts to consider: 2 Esdras (as named in KJV), Psalms of Solomon, Odes of Solomon, and Wisdom of Solomon (in Catholic Bibles). Note how important Solomon tradition was at the time, the ancient wise king son of David. Jesus is presented as "a greater than Solomon" [Matthew 12.42] and as such presents the Sermon on the Mount as the wisest teacher who ever lived.

One interesting preserved statement of cosmopolitan hopes for cross-cultural influence is the Jewish composed text attributed to an Ionic poet: Pseudo-Phocylides. It is in the spirit of such a text that I feel Christianity was conceived, between the spiritual melting pot of Alexandria, the living-out-of-ancient-values in supportive communities of the Dead Sea Scroll people, and the Roman obsession with taking the best of all philosophies and creating a working synthesis.

Christian

The only early Christian text that preserves the Sermon on the Mount is the Gospel of Matthew. It is of interest to explore the parallels between the verses preserved in the gospels of Mark and Luke. The Gospel of John presents a philosophical concept of the word of God in contrast to the world, the light of the world, a comforting spirit to come to reveal the timeless truths, the power of love, oneness with God, retiring to a mountain, non-judgmental forgiveness, and rejection of true prophets by the masses.

A few of the other New Testament writings are included: 1 Corinthians, 1 Peter, 1 Timothy, Galatians, James, Revelation, and Romans. While there are a few occurrences of resonance with these, for the most part the "not here to destroy the Law" of the Sermon on the Mount seems at odds with the "justification by faith alone" of the epistles. Here ends what is included in the Bible, the remainder of the quotes and references being from other writings, Christian and beyond.

The Nag Hammadi Library discovery presented a wealth of early Christian texts that were thought to be long-lost and forgotten. These stand in addition to volumes of New Testament Apocrypha texts. Excluded from the New Testament of the Bible, these thoughts could have been in the minds of the early readers of the Sermon on the Mount: Barnabas, Dialogue of the Saviour, Didache, Pistis Sophia, Shepherd of Hermas, and Thomas. These lights help to complete the picture of what early Christianity meant in terms of the collections of thoughts here woven into the Sermon on the Mount.

Islamic

It may seem out of place to include thoughts from so many centuries after the Sermon on the Mount, but what is found in Muhammad's insights in the Qur'an are resonances with the teachings of Jesus here. It is also fascinating that Islamic Sufi tradition has so many references to Jesus, called Isa in Arabic, that seem to preserve the tone and values of the Sermon on the Mount.

Another Islamic influence for this work is the idea from Muhammad that to every people and in every age there was given a prophet to explain the same truth in whatever way was appropriate.

Pagan

Fundamentalist Christians can reach the "reductio ad absurdum" that all religious thought apart from the Bible and Jewish / Christian tradition is Satanic. This idea goes back to the earliest centuries of Christianity where the "church fathers" strove to present a Christ that was so far superior to the philosophers and gods of the "pagan" world (meaning anything that was not Christian) that even the reading of non-Christian texts was discouraged for Christians. So eventually any knowledge of the resonances of the teachings of Jesus with those of any pagan source was lost.

Homer is touched upon here just as a nod to a couple of ideas presented in his Odyssey. One is Mount Olympus, the home of the Greek gods. While there are noted parallels between the stories of Ulysses / Odysseus and those of Jesus, the exploration of these stands beyond the scope of the discussion on the Sermon on the

Mount. For a Greek audience, the "god man" Jesus who teaches from a mountain to his initiates would remind them of Olympus.

The Stoic Hymn to Zeus serves as a good introduction as to why pagan thought cannot simply be dismissed in a study of early Christianity. If we were not taught otherwise, we could read in this devotion to Father Zeus, to Almighty Jupiter, the same devoted love that Jesus expressed for the God that he calls Father.

Then we come to the Corpus Hermeticum, an ancient collection of instructions from a divine wise teacher on how to connect to God through an ascetic lifestyle. The teacher, Hermes, is identified with the Egyptian god Thoth. The dating of the text is around the second century CE, the same general timeframe for the compiling of early Christian materials. As such, it gives us a unique window into the world from which the Sermon on the Mount and other Christian writings emerged. If it had to sound relevant, contemporary, meaningful and valued, it would have to acknowledge the best of thoughts and visions and frameworks. Perhaps it took until the Gospel of John to fully embrace Logos, but where the Sermon on the Mount stands in simplicity, it does not omit the Hermetic heart, as we note in quoting from this tradition.

Lastly, in the Western pagan world, we come to a story by Philostratus about a holy man named Apollonius of Tyana, said to have lived in the first century CE, the same timeframe presented for the life of Jesus. Apollonius traveled, teaching devotion to God as he said Pythagoras before him had taught, writing letters, influencing officials, healing the sick, exploring a world of spiritual thoughts from the West to the Far East. It is of interest in the present study as to how much his teachings, as presented by Philostratus, resonate with those found in the Sermon on the Mount.

Far Eastern

Five hundred years before Jesus is said to have lived, three thousand miles to the East, there lived a legendary figure, a prince heir to the throne who gave it all up for ascetic pursuits and was revered as being the Awakened One (Buddha) by his disciples. His ideas and influences far surpassed his lifetime and grew to the extent that the king of India, Ashoka Maurya converted to Buddhism and sent out missionaries to the West. While it may be noted that such Eastern influence was felt by Pythagoras and the Neo-Platonists, it is really amazing how many parallels there are with the teachings of Jesus, especially those included in the Sermon on the Mount.

The earliest collections of the teachings of the Buddha are preserved by the Theravada vehicle of Buddhism. The Mahayana vehicle was just beginning at the time Christianity was being formed, and the resonances with thoughts presented stand as interest to us here as well, in the Lotus Sutra and the Tathagata-garbha Sutra. This presents that we all have this hidden Buddha-nature within us that we can free at any time, bringing it forth like shining a light.

As the West is not one tradition, so too the East is not one tradition, and along with Buddhist influence came that of Hindu and Taoist ideas. From the Hindu, we consider the Bhagavad Gita, the teachings of Krishna, manifestation of Vishnu, supreme God in Hindu thought, though guised in a fabric of polytheistic traditions. We also select from the Upanishads, the quest for discovering our oneness with the divine. From the Tao Te Ching we are presented with a choice of following the Way of God as contrasted with the ways of the world.

First Thoughts

Didache 4.1-2 My child, thou shalt remember, day and night, him who speaks the word of God to thee, and thou shalt honour him as the Lord, for where the Lord's nature is spoken of, there is he present. And thou shalt seek daily the presence of the saints, that thou mayest find rest in their words.

Anenjasappaya Sutta 3 Suppose I were to abide with a mind abundant and exalted, having transcended the world and made a firm determination with the mind. When I do so, there will be no more evil unwholesome mental states such as covetousness, ill will, and presumption in me, and with the abandoning of them my mind will be unlimited, immeasurable, and well developed.

From the distant past to the unknown future, from the close and familiar to cultures alien and distant, what if the threads of human thought, or dare we label them "channeled divine thought", expressed in words from languages (some forgotten and dead, some unknown and strange sounding, some yet to come) were woven together into a fabric of a collection of truths that are timeless, that can transcend cultures and ages and remain practical and useful for aeons to come? It would be such a sermon that Jesus would have to have given, one that encapsulates the best of thoughts from the culture and religion at hand as well as reaching outward in space and in time to the best inspired thoughts, to where the resonance is harmonious and it becomes obvious to the recipient of the sermon that every idea of clarity and quality is pointing in the same direction of hope for a better world, for more enlightened compassionate people, for peace, and for a general consensus of awakening.

Bhagavad Gita 16.1-3 Freedom from fear, purity of heart, constancy in sacred learning and contemplation, generosity, self-harmony, adoration, study of the scriptures, austerity, righteousness; non-violence, truth, freedom from anger, renunciation, serenity, aversion to fault-finding, sympathy for all beings, peace from greedy cravings, gentleness, modesty, steadiness; energy, forgiveness, fortitude, purity, a good will, freedom from pride – these are the treasures of the man who is born for heaven.

This very first quote from Krishna christens the ship of our study here, because it is so beautifully and poetically concentrates the Sermon on the Mount into a single sentence.

What are the spiritual treasures? What are the ideas and practices and values that transcend cultures and ages to represent the best conclusions of human thought and observation? What do the mystical strivings of various religious traditions have in common? What is "born again" in the various contexts of religious tradition and culture and age?

Hymn to Zeus

Stoic: Cleanthes' Hymn to Zeus: Most glorious of the immortals, invoked by many names, ever all-powerful, Zeus, the First Cause of Nature, who rules all things with Law, Hail! It is right for mortals to call upon you, since from you we have our being, we whose lot it is to be God's image, we alone of all mortal creatures that live and move upon the earth. Accordingly, I will praise you with my hymn and ever sing of your might. The whole universe, spinning around the earth, goes wherever you lead it and is willingly guided by you. So great is the servant which you hold in your invincible hands, your eternal, two-edged, lightning-forked thunderbolt. By its strokes all the works of nature came to be established, and with it you guide the universal Word of Reason which moves through all creation, mingling with the great sun and the small stars. O God, without you nothing comes to be on earth, neither in the region of the heavenly poles, nor in the sea, except what evil men do in their folly. But you know how to make extraordinary things suitable, and how to bring order forth from chaos; and even that which is unlovely is lovely to you. For thus you have joined all things, the good with the bad, into one, so that the eternal Word of all came to be one. This Word, however, evil mortals flee, poor wretches; though they are desirous of good things for their possession, they neither see nor listen to God's universal Law; and yet, if they obey it intelligently, they would have the good life. But they are senselessly driven to one evil after another: some are eager for fame, no matter how godlessly it is acquired; others are set on making money without any orderly principles in their lives; and others are bent on ease and on the pleasures and delights of the body. They do these foolish things, time and again, and are swept along, eagerly defeating all they really wish for. O Zeus, giver of all, shrouded in dark clouds and holding the vivid bright lightning, rescue men from painful ignorance. Scatter that ignorance far from their hearts, and deign to rule all things in justice, so that, honored in this way, we may render honor to you in return, and sing your deeds unceasingly, as befits mortals; for there is no greater glory for men or for gods than to justly praise the universal Word of Reason.

What if Jesus was the Word of Reason walking among humanity and explaining the Will of the Most Glorious One invoked by the many names? This is a thought the early Greek speaking Christians would have had.

A True Man

Apollonius of Tyana 8.17.23 A true man is needed to see to the ordering of these souls, a God sent by wisdom. Only he has the power to divert them, first from passions to which they are swept with a frenzy too great for normal society, and second from avarice, in which they say they always lack something until they put their lips to a stream of wealth. As for restraining souls from attempting murder, that is perhaps not impossible for such a man, but to absolve them from it is what neither I nor the God who made the world can do.

Jesus presented himself as "son of man", where you would think he would present himself more so as "Son of God", if we view him through the lens of traditional Christianity. It was in this "true man" role that Jesus stood, one of us, facing us, and as such the Sermon on the Mount is presented. There are no great dogmatic assertions in this text, nothing to have blind faith in, not a lot of theology. It is down-to-earth and practical, human advice for humans. Jesus had to present it in this way, echoing back humanity's loftiest ideas, reminding us of the direction we should find ourselves evolving in, affirming our heart-cherished childish dreams of a better world, of peace and love and harmony and forgiveness. He warns us about timeless snares that would impede our progress, for getting us through a world run by lust and greed and violence and mind control. He offers simple freedom in a simple unlearning of how we have found ourselves becoming, a returning to simple values and focused integrity.

Wise Teacher

Udanavarga 4.4 When the wise man dispels heedlessness with heedfulness, on high on the stage of wisdom, he casts his eyes on the sorrowing crowd, the foolish, he the thinker, just as from a mountain height one looks down on those on the plain.

Udanavarga 15.7 You who are awake, listen to me; you who are asleep, wake up. It is better to be awake than asleep; those who are awake have no fear.

Tathagata-garbha Sutra Whether or not buddhas appear in the world, the tathagata-garbha of all beings is eternal and unchanging. It is just that they are covered by kleshas of sentient beings. When the

Tathagata appears in the world, he expounds the Dharma far and wide to remove their ignorance and tribulation and to purify their universal wisdom.

Tathagata-garbha is "Buddha nature", kleshas are unwholesome states of mind. Tathagata (Buddha) with his Dharma, Christ with his Gospel, does not present adding some alien way of thought upon people. People are naturally enlightened, naturally full of light. It is just that we have allowed these unwholesome states of mind to distract us from our true nature. We just need to be reminded of who we are supposed to be, the quality and purpose that is our destinies. In this Buddhist scripture, it was hoped that someone would come along to explain it to humanity in a way that we could easily understand. If by "Tathagata ", the ancient Buddhists meant a perfectly awakened man, then certainly Jesus qualifies to wear the title.

The Sermon on the Mount

Matthew 5.1 And seeing the multitudes, he went up into a mountain: and when he was set, his disciples came unto him:

Matthew 5.2 And he opened his mouth, and taught them, saying,

This was only for the disciples in a private setting, up a mountain, away from the crowds. This does not represent the public ministry of Jesus. It is reserved for those opened to receiving such spiritual truths. Seeing the many, he ran away. He climbed the mountain. Seeing the few who followed him up the mountain, he taught them.

Thomas 62 Jesus said, "It is to those who are worthy of my mysteries that I tell my mysteries. Do not let your left hand know what your right hand is doing."

The ignorant left, left behind crowds, the sheep herd people, will never know what the wise right, right up the mountain disciples, the mountain goat people, will learn from the master.

Expressing the heart of Jewish tradition in a condensed form, from the perspective of Jesus: the blessings of Father Abraham, the mountain peak direct revelation of Moses, and the visionary ideals for a changed world of the prophets are woven together in the Sermon on the Mount. With such promises, insights, and practical instructions, the disciple of Jesus is initiated into a transformed life. It is not an initiation of blind faith, repeated rituals, empty words, or even of religious affiliation. It is an initiation of vision, of purpose, of taking on strong intentions to change. Change is across the spectrum, from changed values, changed speaking, changed acting and interacting, changed goals. As such, this is a spiritual tool that only works when put into practice. It becomes the strong rock foundation that remains strong throughout the storms of life, the inner light that ever shines in the darkest of times, and the sacred salt that protects against even the foulest of mental demons out there.

Abraham Blessings

Genesis 15.1 After these things the word of the Lord came unto Abram in a vision, saying, Fear not, Abram, I am thy shield, and thy exceeding great reward.

The first section of the Sermon on the Mount is about making that connection to God, about positioning yourself in a spiritual place where you are blessed, where synchronicities play out in your daily life, and you understand your own nature and purpose and place in a grander scheme of things.

Abraham was promised descendants that would be rich, conquerors in celebration when they come to rule the world, inherit the earth. In the setting for the Sermon on the Mount, the Jewish Zealots wanted to act upon God's blessings to Abraham, stand together and defeat the Romans who occupied and controlled their land and their lives. They failed in epic ways in the year 70 CE when the Romans recaptured Jerusalem, put an end to the rebellion and destroyed the temple, and then again in the year 135 when the self-proclaimed Messiah Simon ben Kosiba was defeated by the Romans. Hadrian exiled all Jews from Jerusalem, renamed the city Aelia Capitolina, set up a statue of himself at the site where the temple had been destroyed, erected a temple devoted to Jupiter (Father Zeus) at the same site, and erected a temple devoted to Venus. Jews were forbidden to visit the reformed cosmopolitan city

If anyone looked to Jesus to be the Messiah in the traditional sense of being a military commander hero for conquering the known world for the chosen people, they would have been disappointed. His battles were to be fought in the minds of his disciples for a kingdom not observed, with a temple not made by human hands. His, indeed, was a new testament, a new connection to God. Like for Abraham there are blessings and promises and results from establishing this knowledge and acting in accordance with its values and truths.

What blesses you? What empowers magic (miracles, synchronicity, metaphysical synergy, serendipity) for you? What has your back when you are facing the challenges of life? What does it mean to be blessed? Jesus reversed all of the expectations, all of the answers. The blessed are the poor, the meek, the mourning. What is the real inheritance? Who wins the world? Jesus reversed the answers once again. The inheritors are the merciful, the pure in heart, and the peace makers. The heroes of this new vision are the persecuted salt of the earth dedicated to making changes for the better in the world around them, and the hidden away lights of the world who dare to shine their compassion in a world in need of love.

Blessings of God

Psalm 115.12-15 The LORD hath been mindful of us: he will bless us; he will bless the house of Israel; he will bless the house of Aaron. He will bless them that fear the LORD, both small and great. The LORD shall increase you more and more, you and your children. Ye are blessed of the LORD which made heaven and earth.

Psalm 154.16-18 Behold the eyes of the Lord will have compassion upon the good ones; and upon those who glorify him will he increase his mercy; from an evil time will he deliver them. Bless the Lord, who redeems the poor ones from the hand of strangers.

The Militant Poor in Spirit

Dead Sea Scrolls War Scroll 1QM 14.3-8 There they shall all bless the God of Israel and joyously exalt His name together. They shall say in response: "Blessed is the God of Israel, who guards loving-kindness for His covenant and the appointed times of salvation for the people He redeems. He has called those who stumble unto wondrous accomplishments, and He has gathered a congregation of nations for annihilation without remnant in order to raise up in judgment he whose heart has melted, to open a mouth for the dumb to sing God's mighty deeds, and to teach feeble hands warfare. He gives those whose knees shake strength to stand, and strengthens those who have been smitten from the hips to the shoulder. Among the poor in spirit he gives a hard heart, and by those whose way is perfect shall all wicked nations come to an end; there will be no place for all their mighty men. But we are the remnant of your people. Blessed is your name, O God of loving-kindness, the One who kept the covenant for our forefathers.

The "poor in spirit" inheriting the "kingdom of heaven" is tied into the victory of the oppressed people of the covenant over the foreign nations. If there ever was a military origin to the Jesus traditions, it is lost in the way the Sermon on the Mount is presented. If "poor in spirit" is a sectarian reference to the Zealots and their quest for a Messiah / Christ being a great military hero to come and defend the chosen people, it has taken on such a twist here that it actually opposes such a thought.

For the Jesus of the Sermon on the Mount, he teaches and represents attitudes, ideas, values, and ambitions that are directly opposed to the concept of the Messiah / Christ military hero concept. Jesus, is this antidote for, this substitute for, the violence of the failed revolutionaries, occupations, and terrorist activities of the history of the Jewish Zealots in their opposition to the Roman Empire. He presents Jewish Wisdom cleansed of its violent and xenophobic sharp edges.

Blessings of Wisdom

Proverbs 8.32 Now therefore hearken unto me, O ye children: for blessed are they that keep my ways.

Sirach 14.20-21 Blessed is the man that doth meditate good things in wisdom, and that reasoneth of holy things by his understanding. He that considereth her ways in his heart shall also have understanding in her secrets.

Blessed Are the Poor

Matthew 5.3 Blessed are the poor in spirit: for theirs is the kingdom of heaven.

Abu 'Abdallah Ahmad b. Muhammad al-Shaybani Ibn Hanbal: Kitab al-Zuhd 338 Jesus said to his disciples, "In truth I say to you" – and he often used to say, "In truth I say to you" – "those among you who sorrow most in misfortune are the most attached to this world."

"Worldly kingdom" conquered concept stands opposed to "kingdom of heaven" freely obtained, contrasting wealth and power and control with a self-imposed lifestyle of poverty and letting go of worldly concerns. Maybe not "freely", for its cost is a different set of treasure, its "power plays" being all in the mind.

Thomas 54 Jesus said, "Blessed are the poor, for yours is the kingdom of heaven."

Thomas 81 Jesus said, "Let him who has grown rich be king, and let him who possesses power renounce it."

The Thomas collection is interesting in that it presents us with variations of the same thoughts being presented.

Apollonius of Tyana 1.33.1 Apollonius said, "If you had come to my city of Tyana, Majesty, and I was asking you to live where I did, would you do so?" "Certainly not," replied the king, "unless I was going to occupy a house large enough to accommodate my spearmen, my bodyguards, and myself in style." "The same argument holds on my side," said Apollonius. "If my quarters are too good for me, I will be uncomfortably situated, because excess vexes the wise more than deficiency vexes people like you."

Apollonius of Tyana: Letter 77f: The emperor Vespasian greets the philosopher Apollonius. If everyone were willing to be a philosopher of your kind, Apollonius, it would be well both for philosophy and for poverty, since philosophy would be incorruptible and poverty voluntary.

Apollonius of Tyana 1.33.2 [Apollonius said,] "Gods, grant that I have little and need nothing."

Apollonius of Tyana: Letter 35: To Hestiaeus: In my judgement excellence and wealth are direct opposites, since when the one shrinks the other grows, and when one grows the other shrinks. How then is it possible for both to be found in the same person, except by the reasoning of fools, who equate wealth with excellence?

Apollonius of Tyana 7.26.4-5 We mortals are in prison for the whole of the time named "life." This soul of ours is chained to a perishable body, has many sufferings, and is a slave to everything that befalls a human being. Whoever first had the idea of a house seems to me to have enclosed himself in a second prison without knowing it. Why, even those who live in palaces, safely ensconced within them, we may consider to be more confined than those whom they hope to confine. And when I consider cities and their walls, they seem to me communal jails, so that people are imprisoned within them when trading, imprisoned when attending the assembly or the theater or when holding processions.

Apollonius is said to have lived in the same century as Jesus, but he never visited Palestine, not liking the Jewish religion for being so isolated and xenophobic. Nevertheless, his ideas resonate very closely to those of Jesus.

Psalm 37.16 A little that a righteous man hath is better than the riches of many wicked.

James 2.5 Hearken, my beloved brethren, Hath not God chosen the poor of this world rich in faith, and heirs of the kingdom which he hath promised to them that love him?

Udanavarga 2.16 Possessions cause the downfall of the fool, but not of him who seeks by himself. The fool through his possessions and his cravings caused his own downfall as well as that of others.

Monastic vows of poverty range from Buddhist monks and nuns to Pythagorean philosophers to Catholic and Orthodox monks and nuns, all with the same set of values and goals – to escape the "system" at hand in the surrounding culture and live a much simpler lifestyle.

Tao Te Ching 44 A contented man is never disappointed.

Tao Te Ching 46 There is no greater sin than desire, no greater curse than discontent, no greater misfortune than wanting something for oneself. Therefore he who knows that enough is enough will always have enough.

Contentment is key. Values is key. It is really all in the mind.

Abu 'Abdallah Ahmad b. Muhammad al-Shaybani Ibn Hanbal: Kitab al-Zuhd 487 Jesus said, "Satan accompanies the world. His deceit accompanies wealth. His seductiveness accompanies caprice. His ultimate power accompanies the appetites."

'Abdallah al-Marwazi Ibn al-Mubarak: Kitab al-Zuhd wa al-Raqa'iq 284 Jesus said to his disciples, "Just as kings have left wisdom to you, so you should leave the world to them."

Abu 'Abdallah Ahmad b. Muhammad al-Shaybani Ibn Hanbal: Kitab al-Zuhd 320 God revealed to Jesus: "O Jesus, I have granted you the love of the poor and mercy toward them. You love them, and they love you and accept you as their spiritual guide and leader, and you accept them as companions and followers. These are two traits of character. Know that whoever meets me on Judgment Day with these two character traits has met me with the purest of works and the ones most beloved by me."

The Islamic Sufi traditions have a unique insight into Jesus. It always resonates with the heart of the Sermon on the Mount. It was Muhammad's contention that his religion and the religion of Jesus were one and the same. They spoke different languages to different peoples in different times, but they shared the passionate love for the same God.

Love and mercy are the two character traits that will cause you to resonate with God. Each surah (thread) in the Qur'an is opened with "In the name of Allah, most gracious, most merciful."

Meek and Mourning

Isaiah 61.1-2 The Spirit of the Lord GOD is upon me; because the LORD hath anointed me to preach good tidings unto the meek; he hath sent me to bind up the brokenhearted, to proclaim liberty to the captives, and the opening of the prison to them that are bound; To proclaim the acceptable year of the LORD, and the day of vengeance of our God; to comfort all that mourn;

Meek and mourn are grouped here in Isaiah as in Matthew 5.4-5. In the original Hebrew, anointed is MaSHaCH, Messiah.

Psalm 126.4-6 Turn again our captivity, O LORD, as the streams in the south. They that sow in tears shall reap in joy. He that goeth forth and weepeth, bearing precious seed, shall doubtless come again with rejoicing, bringing his sheaves with him.

Sometimes change requires work and dedication before the payoff is observed. There is a breakdown before each quantum leap embrace of change.

Zephaniah 2.3 Seek ye the LORD, all ye meek of the earth, which have wrought his judgment; seek righteousness, seek meekness: it may be ye shall be hid in the day of the LORD'S anger.

Numbers 12.3 (Now the man Moses was very meek, above all the men which were upon the face of the earth.)

Sirach 1.27 For the fear of the Lord is wisdom and instruction: and faith and meekness are his delight.

Sirach 3.17-20 My son, go on with thy business in meekness; so shalt thou be beloved of him that is approved. The greater thou art, the more humble thyself, and thou shalt find favour before the Lord. Many are in high place, and of renown: but mysteries are revealed unto the meek. For the power of the Lord is great, and he is honoured of the lowly.

The Poor, the Remnant, Mourning, the Arrival of God

Amos 5.11-18 Forasmuch therefore as your treading is upon the poor, and ye take from him burdens of wheat: ye have built houses of hewn stone, but ye shall not dwell in them; ye have planted pleasant vineyards, but ye shall not drink wine of them. For I know your manifold transgressions and your mighty sins: they afflict the just, they take a bribe, and they turn aside the poor in the gate from their right. Therefore the prudent shall keep silence in that time; for it is an evil time. Seek good, and not evil, that ye may live: and so the LORD, the God of hosts, shall be with you, as ye have spoken. Hate the evil, and love the good, and establish judgment in the gate: it may be that the LORD God of hosts will be gracious unto the remnant of Joseph. Therefore the LORD, the God of hosts, the Lord, saith thus; Wailing shall be in all streets; and they shall say in all the highways, Alas! alas! and they shall call the husbandman to mourning, and such as are skilful of lamentation to wailing. And in all vineyards shall be wailing: for I will pass through thee, saith the LORD. Woe unto you that desire the day of the LORD! To what end is it for you? The day of the LORD is darkness, and not light.

Blessed Are They That Mourn

Matthew 5.4 Blessed are they that mourn: for they shall be comforted.

Blessed are the sorrowful, knowledge of truth behind the law, redefining what you treasure, and building the house vision, represent the four divisions to the original Sermon on the Mount. Krishna supplies the outline [Bhagavad Gita 7.16]: 1. The man of sorrows (blessed are, life experiences), 2. The seeker of Gnosis (hidden meaning of the Law, religion), 3. The seeker of treasure (presentations, values, spirituality), and 4. The visionary (shining a light, building a path, building a house, Gnosticism).

To sorrow, to mourn, to redefine values, shift paradigm, unplug from what the world out there wants you to want and identify with and think about and react to. Their way now seems poison to you, their values worthless to you. This is the comfort of those blessed enough to mourn, to follow their heart to seek out a different treasure.

Bhagavad Gita 7.16 There are four kind of men who are good, and the four love me, Arjuna: the man of sorrows, the seeker of knowledge, the seeker of something he treasures, and the man of vision.

These four provide the framework for the Sermon on the Mount. It begins here with "sorrows", the turning of one's back on the riches and fame and comforts of the world as being the answer. This vacuum is then filled with a quest for knowledge of what does really matter, then of seeking out this treasure, and by this change of heart to come to have a vision that is alien to the surrounding world. From the perspective of the mountain top, the disciples have a vision that the crowds back down in the city cannot understand or appreciate.

Devaputtasamyutta 18 I hope that you're untroubled, bhikkhu. I hope no delight is found in you. I hope that when you sit all alone discontent doesn't spread over you. Truly, I'm untroubled, spirit, yet no delight is found in me. And when I'm sitting all alone discontent doesn't spread over me. How are you untroubled, bhikkhu? How is no delight found in you? How come, when you sit all alone, discontent doesn't spread over you? Delight comes to one who is miserable, misery to one filled with delight.

Bhikkhu means disciple, initiate, student, hoping for arriving at that aha moment where it all makes sense, it all works. Buddha was about training his bhikkhus. Christ was about training his disciples. It was not important that the bhikkhus had a passion for the Buddha, only that they in their own personal lives and minds partook of the message, embraced it, lived it out. In what way is being a disciple of Christ like being a bhikkhu of Buddha?

It is a vicious cycle – you are depressed, you seek comfort in something, but it just leaves you more depressed. Buddha suggests we break the chain, uncomplicate our lives. The mourning can't just be for superficial wants – riches, mates, security. What is spiritual craving to fill a spiritual void? What is a mourning that can only be satisfied with the comforting arrival of the Spiritual Answer.

Inheriting the Earth

Psalm 37.9-11 For evildoers shall be cut off: but those that wait upon the LORD, they shall inherit the earth. For yet a little while, and the wicked shall not be: yea, thou shalt diligently consider his place, and it shall not be. But the meek shall inherit the earth; and shall delight themselves in the abundance of peace.

20

AL ANBIYA 21.105 Before this We wrote in the Psalms, after the Message (given to Moses): My servants the righteous, shall inherit the earth."

Dead Sea Scrolls 4Q171 2.5-11 "Very soon there will be no wicked man; I look where he was, he's not there". This refers to all of the wicked at the end of the forty years. When those years are completed, there will no longer be on the earth any wicked person. "Then the meek will inherit the earth and enjoy all the abundance that peace brings". This refers to the company of the poor who endure the time of error but are delivered from all the snares of Belial. Afterwards they will enjoy all the fruits of the earth and grow fat on every human luxury.

Psalm 25.4-14 Shew me thy ways, O LORD; teach me thy paths. Let me in thy truth, and teach me: for thou are the God of my salvation; on thee do I wait all the day. Remember, O LORD, thy tender mercies and they lovingkindnesses; for they have been ever of old. Remember not the sins of my youth, nor my transgressions: according to thy mercy remember thou me for thy goodness sake, O LORD. Good and upright is the LORD: therefore will he teach sinners in the way. The meek will he guide in judgment: and the meek will he teach his way. All the paths of the LORD are mercy and truth unto such as keep his covenant and his testimonies. For thy name's sake, O LORD, pardon mine iniquity; for it is great. What man is he that feareth the LORD? Him shall he teach in the way that he shall choose. His soul shall dwell at ease; and his seed shall inherit the earth. The secret of the LORD is with them that fear him; and he will shew them his covenant.

The way I think about these verses is: "Show me the way, the truth, and the salvation (YeSHaH / Jesus); remind me of the eternal loving-kindnesses (CHeSeD). Don't see me for my foolish transgressions of youth, but according to your mercy (CHeSeD) think of me in terms of your goodness. You are only goodness, and wish to teach sinners your way. The meek will you guide in judgment: and the meek will you teach your way. You only travel paths of mercy (CHeSeD) and remain true to those who value your revelations and your prophets. You will show me the way you choose for me, leaving my mind at rest and my body inheriting your world, showing me all your secrets."

Salvation and love, YeSHaH and CheSeD in Hebrew, define Christianity in that "Jesus" means salvation and "God is love" is one of the lasting themes of early Christian thought. God is mercy. God is compassion. God is kindness. God is empathy. God is comforting. This is a change from God being represented as wanting war, wanting to destroy the foreign enemy, wanting judgment. This is challenging that whole religious mindset.

Psalm 37.18 The LORD knoweth the days of the upright: and their inheritance shall be for ever.

Psalm 37.22 For such as be blessed of him shall inherit the earth; and they that be cursed of him shall be cut off.

Psalm 37.29 The righteous shall inherit the land, and dwell therein for ever.

Isaiah 49.8 Thus saith the LORD, In an acceptable time have I heard thee, and in a day of salvation have I helped thee: and I will preserve thee, and give thee for a covenant of the people, to establish the earth, to cause to inherit the desolate heritages;

The way I think about this verse is: "This is a day of salvation [YeSHuW'aH, Joshua, Jesus], of help and preservation and renewed covenant, a rededication of the whole planet, a remembering of the inheritance due to the desolate."

The "poor" are key in the message of Jesus because we are all the poor, and we are all the rich. We all are set to inherit a great wealth, but we don't remember anything about it. In the Acts of Thomas, there is a parable about a prince who got lost in the world of Egypt and forgot he was a prince. We have to wake up, remember, and take our place as rightful heirs to everything God can resonate within our lives.

1 Samuel 2.8 He raiseth up the poor out of the dust, and lifteth up the beggar from the dunghill, to set them among princes, and to make them inherit the throne of glory: for the pillars of the earth are the LORD'S, and he hath set the world upon them.

Jubilees 32.19 And I shall give to your seed all of the land under heaven and they will rule in all nations as they have desired. And after this all of the earth will be gathered together and they will inherit it forever.

1 Enoch 96.1 Be hopeful, you righteous ones, for the sinners shall soon perish from before your presence. You shall be given authority upon them, such authority as you may wish to have.

The times change. Where once the world was a frontier where the physically strong bullied the physically weak and this defined order, change comes and the world becomes a more sophisticated place where the intellectuals are the important ones and brute strength no longer rules. It is a conquering through reason instead of through violence.

AL NUR 24.55 Allah has promised, to those among you who believe and work righteous deeds, that He will, of a surety, grant them in the land, inheritance (of power), as He granted it to those before them; that He will establish in authority their religion – the one which He has chosen for them; and that He will change (their state), after the fear in which they (lived), to one of security and peace: 'They will worship Me (alone) and not associate aught with Me. 'If any do reject Faith after this, they are rebellious and wicked.

It is inevitable that reasonableness will one day be the norm.

MARYAM 19.40 It is We Who will inherit the earth, and all beings thereon: to Us will they all be returned.

This "inheriting the earth" thread reaches from Judaism to Islam. It is a dream for a better world of peace without oppression, safe and pure for those who want to build happy families, communities, nations, and a planet where everyone looks out for each other in the spirit of empathy and charity and mutual responsibility.

As the ancient Jews found out, Messianic dreams of violent revolution is not the answer. As Christianity should reflect upon, crusades and inquisitions were not the answer. Islam today needs desperately to conclude that the answer lies not in acts of terrorism and military might. Change must indeed come to the world, but the method of change needs to be heart-driven instead of violence-driven.

Blessed Are the Meek

Matthew 5.5 Blessed are the meek: for they shall inherit the earth.

Matthew 5.6 Blessed are they which do hunger and thirst after righteousness: for they shall be filled.

It is this hunger for a better world that will eventually fill the whole world with justice, with peace, with elimination of prejudice, with elimination of neglect.

Barnabas 19.3 Thou shalt not exalt thyself, but shalt be lowly minded in all things. Thou shalt not assume glory to thyself. Thou shalt not entertain a wicked design against thy neighbor; thou shalt not admit boldness into thy soul.

James 4.10 Humble yourselves in the sight of the Lord, and he shall lift you up.

Didache 3.5-7 My child, be not a liar, for lying leads to theft, nor a lover of money, nor vain-glorious, for from all these things are thefts engendered. My child, be not a grumbler, for this leads to blasphemy, nor stubborn, nor a thinker of evil, for from all these are blasphemies engendered, but be thou "meek, for the meek shall inherit the earth;"

Khandhasamyutta 76 Having reached the stage of the tamed, they are the victors in the world. Above, across, and below, delight is no more found in them. They boldly sound their lion's roar: The enlightened are supreme in the world.

Tao Te Ching 36 Soft and weak overcome hard and strong.

Tao Te Ching 78 Under heaven nothing is more soft and yielding than water. Yet for attacking the solid and strong, nothing is better; it has no equal. The weak can overcome the strong; the supple can overcome the stiff.

LUQMAN 31.18 "And swell not thy cheek (for pride) at men, nor walk in insolence through the earth; for Allah loveth not any arrogant boaster.

Abu 'Abdallah Ahmad b. Muhammad al-Shaybani Ibn Hanbal: Kitab al-Zuhd 312 Jesus said, "Why do I not observe in you the best of worship?" They said, "What is the best of worship, Spirit of God?" He said, "Humility before God."

Merciful, Pure Heart, Peacemaker

Psalm 85.7-13 Shew us thy mercy, O LORD, and grant us thy salvation. I will hear what God the LORD will speak: for he will speak peace unto his people, and to his saints: but let them not turn again to folly. Surely his salvation is nigh them that fear him; that glory may dwell in our land. Mercy and truth are met together; righteousness and peace have kissed each other. Truth shall spring out of the earth; and righteousness shall look down from heaven. Yea, the LORD shall give that which is good; and our land shall yield her increase.

Righteousness shall go before him; and shall set us in the way of his steps.

The way I think about these verses is: "Revealed mercy (CHeSeD), granted salvation (YeSHaH / Jesus), peace unto his people, sanctification and protection from being led once again into folly, means that salvation (YeSHaH / Jesus) is near, and glory enlightening our land. Mercy (CHeSeD) and truth are married together; justice and peace gently embrace. Truth shall grow from the earth; and righteousness shall shine down from heaven." These verses are ripe with symbolism used in the Sermon on the Mount.

It should be contemplated that "Jesus", as a name, and as the teacher of this Sermon on the Mount, is the very personification of "Salvation", the very representative of "salvation" of the God of "CHeSeD". The meaning of the name would have been obvious to the early Christians, but it is obscured in English. What is the Message of God? What does the Word of God have to say to humanity? What would he have us grow from our dirt? What would he have us witness from our sky?

Svetasvatara Upanishad 4 In the vision of this God of love there is everlasting peace.

This Hindu quote illustrates that love and peace are the dream of many diverse peoples. When it becomes the overpowering dream of most of humanity, then what will the world be like?

Blessed Are the Merciful

Matthew 5.7 Blessed are the merciful: for they shall obtain mercy.

Matthew 5.8 Blessed are the pure in heart: for they shall see God.

Matthew 5.9 Blessed are the peacemakers: for they shall be called the children of God.

Didache 3.8 Be thou long-suffering, and merciful and guileless, and quiet, and good, and ever fearing the words which thou hast heard.

Psalm 15.1-3 <A Psalm of David.> LORD, who shall abide in thy tabernacle? who shall dwell in thy holy hill? He that walketh uprightly, and worketh righteousness, and speaketh the truth in his heart. He that backbiteth not with his tongue, nor doeth evil to his neighbour, nor taketh up a reproach against his neighbour.

Dead Sea Scrolls 4Q525 Frag 2 2.1-7 Blessed is the one who [...] with a clean heart and does not slander with his tongue. Blessed are those who hold fast to its statutes and do not hold fast to the ways of injustice. Blessed are those who rejoice in it, and do not burst forth on paths of folly. Blessed are those who seek it with pure hands, and do not search for it with a deceitful heart. Blessed is the man who attains wisdom, and walks in the law of the Most High: establishes his heart in its ways, restrains himself by its corrections, is continually satisfied with its punishments, does not forsake it in the face of his trials, at the time of distress he does not abandon it, does not forget it in the day of terror, and in the humility of his soul he does not abhor it. But he meditates on it continually, and in his trial he reflects on the law, and with all his being he gains understanding in it, and he establishes it before his eyes so as not to walk in the ways of injustice.

In this way of thinking, there is a sense of free will at play here. Blessed are those who choose to be good. No one is predestined to be evil and are thus beyond hope. It comes down to choice. There is no justification by blind faith alone. The faith must be put into practice.

AL BAQARAH 2.193 And fight them on until there is no more Tumult or oppression, and there prevail justice and faith in Allah; but if they cease, let there be no hostility except to those who practise oppression.

Winning the battle is not about showing no mercy. Fighting oppression as a righteous cause ends when the enemy is no longer a threat. Peace should be the ultimate goal – oppression ceased.

Bhagavad Gita 2.38 Prepare for war with peace in thy soul. Be in peace in pleasure and pain, in gain and in loss, in victory or in the loss of a battle. In this peace there is no sin.

Blessed are the peacemakers, or is it rather those who prepare for war with peace in their hearts? There is no definition of peace apart from absence of violence. Everyone has an agenda, winning the next great objective, advancing the cause of the moment. To face the battle with an inner peace is profound. Make the very definition of victory for you be the fact that you retain this inner peace, this composure, this celestial bliss of perfection in the midst of life in the mundane world of disasters and problems. This isn't an apathy. This isn't a weakness. This is where peace is the ultimate value, stronger than revenge, stronger than hate, stronger than xenophobia.

Blessed Are The Persecuted

Matthew 5.10 Blessed are they which are persecuted for righteousness' sake: for theirs is the kingdom of heaven.

Matthew 5.11 Blessed are ye, when men shall revile you, and persecute you, and shall say all manner of evil against you falsely, for my sake.

Matthew 5.12 Rejoice, and be exceeding glad: for great is your reward in heaven: for so persecuted they the prophets which were before you.

John 17.14-17 I have given them thy word; and the world hath hated them, because they are not of the world, even as I am not of the world. I pray not that thou shouldest take them out of the world, but that thou shouldest keep them from the evil. They are not of the world, even as I am not of the world. Sanctify them through thy truth: thy word is truth.

Thomas 68 Jesus said, "Blessed are you when you are hated and persecuted. Wherever you have been persecuted they will find no place."

Karma plays out in the end. Places that persecute good people will eventually be erased from the map. All oppressive governments are eventually overthrown. Eventually it all ends, the witch hunts, slavery, crusades, inquisitions, discrimination, bullying. Think of all those in the past persecuted for being of a different race, segregation laws, internment camps, the taking of native lands. Eventually these things are no more. Imagine a world that doesn't persecute differences? Imagine a world safe for homosexuals, safe for atheists, safe for drug users? How far can we extend not being persecuted?

Thomas 69 Jesus said, "Blessed are they who have been persecuted within themselves. It is they who have truly come to know the father. Blessed are the hungry, for the belly of him who desires will be filled."

Sometimes different is just ahead of the rest of the world. It is the smart kid that gets beaten by the bully. It is the visionary that gets laughed at by those thinking inside the old box.

Khandhasamyutta 94 Bhikkus, just as a blue, red, or white lotus is born in the water and grows up in the water, but having risen up above the water, it stands unsullied by the water, so too the Tathagata was born in the world and grew up in the world, but having overcome the world, he dwells unsullied by the world.

Sometimes you stand with values that the world around you doesn't appreciate.

Lotus Sutra 13 In an evil age there will be many things to fear. Evil demons will take possession of others and through them curse, revile and heap shame on us. But we, reverently trusting in the Buddha will put on the armor of perseverance. In order to preach this sutra we will bear these difficult things. We care nothing for our bodies or lives but are anxious only for the unsurpassed way.

If we replace "Buddha" with "Christ" and "sutra" with "gospel" the sentiments are very much at home in early Christianity. Replace with "Prophet" and "Qur'an" and the sentiments are very much at home in early Islam. We, as humans, have the same basic ideals, the same discovered truths, but according to our language and culture, we use different words to express them.

YA SIN 36.30 Ah! Alas for (My) Servants! There comes not a messenger to them but they mock him!

This has been noted across ages and cultures and languages – those with insight are rejected by the herd.

YA SIN 36.10 The same is it to them whether thou admonish them or thou do not admonish them: they will not believe.

AL SHU'ARA 26.117 He said: "O my Lord! Truly my people have rejected me.

FATIR 35.4 And if they reject thee, so were messengers rejected before thee: to Allah go back for decision all affairs.

FATIR 35.25 And if they reject thee, so did their predecessors, to whom came their messengers with Clear Signs, Books of dark prophecies, and the Book of Enlightenment.

AL HIJR 15.10-11 We did send messengers before thee amongst the religious sects of old: but never came a messenger to them but they mocked him.

Buddha was a heretic from the perspective of Hinduism. Jesus was a heretic from the perspective of Judaism. Abraham was a heretic from the perspective of polytheism.

FATIR 35.42 They swore their strongest oaths by Allah that if a warner came to them, they would follow his guidance better than any (other) of the Peoples: But when a warner came to them, it has only increased their flight (from righteousness).

This is a timeless truth, a constant across cultures and ages. Those with insight and vision for needed change are met with opposition from those wanting to keep things the same. The kings opposed democracy. The religious institution opposed science. The war machine opposed peace. The true prophets, the visionaries for change, have to carry on.

Salt

Matthew 5.13 Ye are the salt of the earth: but if the salt have lost his savour, wherewith shall it be salted? it is thenceforth good for nothing, but to be cast out, and to be trodden under foot of men.

Leviticus 2.13 And every oblation of thy meat offering shalt thou season with salt; neither shalt thou suffer the salt of the covenant of thy God to be lacking from thy meat offering: with all thine offerings thou shalt offer salt.

Numbers 18.19 All the heave offerings of the holy things, which the children of Israel offer unto the LORD, have I given thee, and thy sons and thy daughters with thee, by a statute for ever: it is a covenant of salt for ever before the LORD unto thee and to thy seed with thee.

The concept of the holiness of a people being considered a "living sacrifice" was introduced in the Dead Sea Scrolls. The pure people make up for an impure world. This is the building of a rock foundation that will survive the storms of the world. While Christian theology reads this "stone" as being a reference to Christ, the Dead Sea Scrolls society (the Yahad) saw this as a reference to a community of sacred minded people.

Isaiah 28.16 Therefore thus saith the Lord God, Behold, I lay in Zion for a foundation a stone, a tried stone, a precious corner stone, a sure foundation, he that believeth shall not make haste.

Dead Sea Scrolls Community Rule 1QS 8.1-10 In the society of the Yahad there shall be twelve laymen and three priests who are blameless in the light of all that has been revealed from the whole Law, so as to work truth, righteousness, justice, loving-kindness, and humility, one with another. They are to preserve faith in the land with self-control and a broken spirit, atoning for sin by working justice and suffering affliction. They are to walk with all by the standard of truth and the dictates proper to the age. When such men as these come to be in Israel, then shall the society of the Yahad truly be established, an "eternal planting", a temple for Israel, and – mystery! – a Holy of Holies for Aaron; true witnesses to justice, chosen by God's will to atone for the land and to recompense the wicked their due. They will be "the tested wall, the precious cornerstone" whose foundation shall neither be shaken nor swayed, a fortress, a Holy of Holies for Aaron, all of them knowing the Covenant of Justice and thereby offering a sweet savor. They shall be a blameless and true house in Israel, upholding the covenant of eternal statutes. They shall be an acceptable sacrifice, atoning for the land and ringing in the verdict against evil, so that perversity ceases to exist.

The twelve laymen (twelve Apostles?) and three priests (Peter and James and John?) pose an interesting question of just how closely the Jesus tradition fits in with the Dead Sea Scrolls' sectarian community, the "Yahad" (Unity). It is beyond the scope of this book to explore. What is interesting in light of the Sermon on the Mount is the concepts of the sacred being redefined in terms of living people offering the sacrifice of holy lives superseding the old religion of animal sacrifices in a temple building. So what then becomes the required "salt" for such a living sacrifice?

It is interesting that the "salt" for a "living sacrifice" was defined as Sophia (Wisdom) in the Gospel of Philip. It is this salting that makes the "living sacrifice" to be accepted by God.

Philip 2.59.27-29 The apostles said to the disciples, "May our entire offering obtain salt." They called Sophia "salt." Without it no offering is acceptable."

This is the first of a select few verses from Matthew's Sermon on the Mount that appears in Mark's gospel (Mark 9.50). Apart from the core of the "how do you re-salt unsalty salt" koan, the three versions are different. Mark introduces the concept of salt having to do with sacrifice and then proceeds to suggest that we all have such salt present to live in peace, supposedly meaning to live a life of self-sacrifice and service. Matthew's verse is perhaps more prophetic, as if the "salt of the earth" Jews were about to become outcasts and overrun by footsteps of foreigners. Luke combines the two in a harmony (Luke 14.34-35) that leaves the meaning blurry except for those who happen to have ears to hear.

'Abdallah al-Marwazi Ibn al-Mubarak: Kitab al-Zuhd wa al-Raqa'iq 283 Jesus said to his disciples, "Do not take wages from those whom you teach, except such wages as you gave me. Salt of the earth, do not become corrupt. Everything when it becomes corrupt can be treated with salt, but if salt is corrupted it has no remedy. Know that you possess two traits of ignorance: laughter without cause for wonder, and morning nap without wakefulness."

Thomas 28 Jesus said, "I took my place in the midst of the world, and I appeared to them in flesh. I found all of them intoxicated; I found none of them thirsty. And my soul became afflicted for the sons of men, because they are blind in their hearts and do not have sight; for empty they came into the world, and empty too they seek to leave the world. But for the moment they are intoxicated. When they shake off their wine, then they will repent."

Being a drunk makes you laugh without having accomplished anything worth being happy over, and it makes you sleep the day away. The hope for the world, the potentially "enlightened" ones, have too much to actually accomplish to become drunks. Drunk on business profits, drunk on diversions, drunk on the luxuries of life, life passes by as we go through the motions like zombies, failing to accomplish anything worth leaving behind.

Eternal Flame

Matthew 5.14 Ye are the light of the world. A city that is set on an hill cannot be hid.

Thomas 24 His disciples said to him, "Show us the place where you are, since it is necessary for us to seek it." He said to them, "Whoever has ears, let him hear. There is light within a man of light, and he lights up the whole world. If he does not shine, he is darkness."

Thomas 32 Jesus said, "A city being built on a high mountain and fortified cannot fall, nor can it be hidden."

2 Kings 8.19 Yet the LORD would not destroy Judah for David his servant's sake, as he promised him to give him alway a light, and to his children.

2 Chronicles 21.7 Howbeit the LORD would not destroy the house of David, because of the covenant that he had made with David, and as he promised to give a light to him and to his sons for ever.

Exodus 27.20 And thou shalt command the children of Israel, that they bring thee pure oil olive beaten for the light, to cause the lamp to burn always.

We are this generation's light sources. If we don't shine, we live in a darkened world. We can't just sit back and hope some governmental institution out there is going to step in and help. We can't just sit back and wait for some religious institution to jump in. We have the light within each of us. We have the ability to become the light source of hope and empathy and assistance in a world of need.

Isaiah 42.16 And I will bring the blind by a way that they knew not; I will lead them in paths that they have not known: I will make darkness light before them, and crooked things straight. These things will I do unto them, and not forsake them.

Sirach 20.30-31 & 41.14-15 Wisdom that is hid, and treasure that is hoarded up, what profit is in them both? Better is he that hideth his folly than a man that hideth his wisdom.

1 Enoch 38.4 And from that time, those who possess the earth will neither be rulers nor princes, they shall not be able to behold the faces of the holy ones, for the light of the Lord of the Spirits has shined upon the face of the holy, the righteous, and the elect.

1 Enoch 50.1 In those days, there will be a change for the holy and the righteous ones and the light of days shall rest upon them; and glory and honor shall be given back to the holy ones, on the day of weariness.

What if good actually did win? A world of charity, mutual respect, the celebration of diversities, brotherhood of man concept becoming the new normal in the world? What if good wasn't just the ideas of those too different to fit in with and buy into the corrupt and greedy world system at play in human politics and culture and religion and media? What if good became the new standard?

Odes of Solomon 25.7 A lamp you set for me both on my right and on my left, so that there might not be in me anything that is not light.

Nothing to hide from coming to light, no secrets, no hidden agendas, but just open honesty remains to be seen.

John 9.5 As long as I am in the world, I am the light of the world.

Let it Shine

Matthew 5.15 Neither do men light a candle, and put it under a bushel, but on a candlestick; and it giveth light unto all that are in the house.

Thomas 33 Jesus said, "Preach from your housetops that which you will hear in your ear. For no one lights a lamp and puts it under a bushel, nor does he put it in a hidden place, but rather he sets it on a lampstand so that everyone who enters and leaves will see its light."

Mark 4.21 And he said unto them, Is a candle brought to be put under a bushel, or under a bed? And not to be set on a candlestick?

Sirach 4.23-24 And refrain not to speak, when there is occasion to do good, and hide not thy wisdom in her beauty. For by speech wisdom shall be known: and learning by the word of the tongue.

Anuruddha Sutta 16 Suppose an oil-lamp is burning with pure oil and a pure wick; because of the purity of its oil and its wick it does not burn dimly. So too, here a bhikkhu abides resolved upon and pervading an area with a pure radiance. His bodily inertia has fully subsided, his sloth and torpor have been fully eliminated, his restlessness and remorse have been fully removed; because of this he meditates, as it were, brightly. On the dissolution of the body, after death, he reappears in the company of the gods of Pure Radiance.

It should be obvious that this becoming a light source is also a Buddhist concept. So many missionaries being sent to Asia to convert those who think in Buddhist terms to think instead in Christian terms could benefit from understanding just how closely Jesus and Siddhartha Gautama Buddha thought. For their differences in 500 years and 3000 miles, it is remarkable how much their thoughts resonate. In this harmonious statement of vision and direction of hope, we find the sacred that transcends cultures, transcends religions, and transcends ages.

Vatthupama Sutta 21, Mahavacchagotta Sutta 15 Master Gautama has made the Dharma clear in many ways, as though he were turning upright what had been overthrown, revealing what was hidden, showing the way to one who was lost, or holding up a lamp in the dark for those with eyesight to see forms.

It is in finding quotes like this one from the Buddhist scriptures that triggered my wondering as to just how related Christianity could be to Buddhism, how inspired, how influenced. In this one quote is referenced the standing up of a fallen lamp, the way, the lost, and having eyes to see such miracles at play. Such concentrated resonance should be able to be found between the gospels and Jewish scriptures, but the observation remains that a tighter resonance is found between the gospels and Buddhist scriptures in many cases.

Brahmanasamyutta 9 When kindling wood, Brahmin, do not imagine this external deed brings purity; for experts say no purity is gained by one who seeks it outwardly. Having given up the fire made from wood, I kindle, O Brahmin, the inner light alone. Always ablaze, my mind always concentrated, I am an arahant living the holy life.

Bhikkhusamyutta 7 When the wise man is in the midst of fools they do not know him if he does not speak, but they know him when he speaks, pointing out the deathless state. He should speak and explain the Dharma, he should raise high the seers' banner. Well-spoken words are the seers' banner: for the Dharma is the banner of seers.

Buddha speaks of "Dharma" like Jesus speaks of "Kingdom", like Christians speak of "Gospel". It is the truth being carried around and expressed in choices, in interactions, in values, and in ideals.

Iddhipadasamyutta 20 A bhikkhu, with a mind that is open and unenveloped, develops the mind imbued with luminosity.

An open mind that can think outside the box shines the brightest.

Lotus Sutra 21 After the Thus Come One has passed into extinction, this person will know the sutras (threads) preached by the Buddha, their causes and conditions and their proper sequence, and will preach them truthfully in accordance with principle. As the light of the sun and moon can banish all obscurity and gloom, so this person as he passes through the world can wipe out the darkness of living beings, causing immeasurable numbers of bodhisattvas in the end to dwell in the single vehicle.

Bodhisattvas is an interesting Buddhist concept. The heart of it is that one who takes this vow becomes obsessed with enlightening as many as possible. The Christian equivalent is perhaps that of being a missionary. Vehicle refers to a specific religious tradition, a means to spiritually advancing. The thought here in the Lotus Sutra is that one day we will all think of ourselves as belonging to the one all-embracing vehicle. There is this Fundamentalist fright to the words "one world religion" as if this would undermine their unique tradition's special values. The end result, perhaps in hundreds of more years, will be that whatever unique values lie in each of the world's spiritual traditions will become embraced by all. What values could these be but those expressed here in the Sermon on the Mount and in the ideas from the various traditions that so beautifully resonate here?

Bhagavad Gita 6.21-22 Then the seeker knows the joy of Eternity: a vision seen by reason far beyond what senses can see. He abides therein and moves not from Truth. He has found joy and Truth, a vision for him supreme. He is therein steady: the greatest pain moves him not.

AL BAQARAH 2.42 And cover not Truth with falsehood, nor conceal the Truth when ye know (what it is).

Keep it real and honest and open and tell it like it is. There is a great deal of Energy in this way of being, and Energy that will bless and empower and align. Shining a light can at first be painful. It can illuminate what is ugly, what is wrong, what needs to be changed. The answer is not to remain in dark denial. The answer is to shine the light and then get to work if so needed.

AL 'IMRAN 3.104 Let there arise out of you a band of people inviting to all that is good, enjoining what is right, and forbidding what is wrong: They are the ones to attain felicity.

Mundaka Upanishad 2 Radiant in his light, yet invisible in the secret place of the heart, the Spirit is the supreme above wherein dwells all that moves and breathes and sees.

We are the eyes through which God looks at our lives. We are the hands through which God then works to improve the vision.

Let Your Light So Shine

Matthew 5.16 Let your light so shine before men, that they may see your good works, and glorify your Father which is in heaven.

1 John 4.4 Ye are of God, little children, and have overcome them: because greater is he that is in you, than he that is in the world.

The real origin of any sense of light or inner joy or unbreakable peace is the God you have connected to within. The distractions for God out there in the world of human religions, cultures, politics, economics, media, tradition, these substitutes block the connection to the true God found within your heart.

Matthew 17.2 And was transfigured before them: and his face did shine as the sun, and his raiment was white as the light.

The ultimate let your light shine. Ever meet a truly happy person? They glow.

Bhagavad Gita 2.3 Fall not into degrading weakness, for this becomes not a man who is a man. Throw off this ignoble discouragement, and arise like a fire that burns all before it.

Bhagavad Gita 3.26 Let not the wise disturb the mind of the unwise in their selfish work. Let him, working with devotion, show them the joy of good work.

This letting light shine is like the arisen fire that fights off the weakness of discouragement and provides a baptism of fire for all who cross its path. Ever meet someone so holy that the encounter changes you? What if you became such a person?

Tathagata-garbha Sutra When I regard all beings with my Buddha (awakened) cakshur (eye), I see that hidden within the kleshas (unwholesome states of mind) of raga (greed), lobha (confusion), dvesha (hatred) and moha (obscuration) there is seated augustly and unmovingly the Tathagata (Buddha) jnana (gnosis / experience), the Tathagata-vision and the Tathagata kaya (light body).

Within us all, deeper than our surface states of mind, exists this light, this true nature, this inner Holy Spirit that we need to focus upon past the noise of the distractions of our acquired reactionary responses of self-interests. This is a force we can directly experience, a fire we can personally kindle, a presence we can tangibly produce.

For the initiated disciples of Jesus, this is one of his initial instructions: Connect to this inner source through gnosis (direct personal experience). In short, to be blessed by God in itself becomes a blessing for others, making the one who is thus blessed to be a helper, an instructor, a guide, an understanding friend.

St. John of the Cross: Spiritual Canticle 31.1 The soul is like the peg on which the garlands are hung, since she is the subject of this glory and no longer appears to be what she was before. But by the perfection and beauty of all the flowers, she resembles the perfect flower Himself. This thread of love joins and binds God and the soul so strongly that it unites and transforms them. So great is this union that even though they differ in substance, in glory and appearance the soul seems to be God and God seems to be the soul.

Moses Laws

Having a good heart fulfills the very purpose for there being laws. If you love peace and serenity, you naturally oppose violence, reach across divisions, and even reach out to adversaries. If you love domestic bliss, you naturally shun acting on feelings of lust that would divide happy couples, avoid adultery, work to prevent divorce and disharmony. If you cherish reason and sanity, you avoid being led around by superstitious nonsense, and rigid inflexible mindsets that lead to prejudice.

The Jesus stories were not designed to invalidate the scriptures of the Jewish Torah (Law) and the Jewish Prophets. By reading the "inspiration" verses alongside the gospel material, it is evident that the gospel encapsulated the "best of" ideas from the collections of Jewish texts, condensed the concepts into simple and easy to remember events and parables that could be passed along as folk stories to the people. In the Marcion and Luke attempts to make the gospel more "Paul" style, Jewish scripture references were removed or obscured to present a Jesus that lived and taught a "new testament" that superseded the "old testament" of Jewish scriptures. "Good works" was replaced with "justification by faith" and the study of Law and Prophets was replaced with the collection of Epistles of Paul along with a gospel (Luke) that was redacted away from its Jewish roots. The Sermon on the Mount preserves an earlier Christianity, one not as anti-Jewish as in later centuries.

James 2.10-14 For whosoever shall keep the whole law, and yet offend in one point, he is guilty of all. For he that said, Do not commit adultery, said also, Do not kill. Now if thou commit no adultery, yet if thou kill, thou art become a transgressor of the law. So speak ye, and so do, as they that shall be judged by the law of liberty. For he shall have judgment without mercy, that hath shewed no mercy; and mercy rejoiceth against judgment. What doth it profit, my brethren, though a man say he hath faith, and have not works? can faith save him?

When did religion get to be about what you have agreed to believe in (blind faith) instead of what you directly experience (gnosis) and put into practice in your daily life? When did religion become a noun instead of a verb?

Deuteronomy 28.9 The LORD shall establish thee an holy people unto himself, as he hath sworn unto thee, if thou shalt keep the commandments of the LORD thy God, and walk in his ways.

Dead Sea Scrolls Community Rule 1QS 1.1-9 A text belonging to the Instructor, who is to teach the Holy Ones how to live according to the book of the Yahad. He is to teach them to seek God with all their heart and with all their soul, to do that which is good and upright before Him, just as He commanded through Moses and all His servants the prophets. He is to teach them to love everything He chose and to hate everything He rejected, to distance themselves from all evil and to hold fast to all good deeds; to practice truth, justice, and righteousness in the land, and to walk no longer in a guilty, willful heart and lustful desires, wherein they did every evil thing. He is to induct all who volunteer to live by the laws of God into the Covenant of Mercy, so as to be joined to God's society and walk faultless before Him, according to all that has been revealed for the times appointed them.

Isaiah 33.6 And wisdom and knowledge shall be the stability of thy times, and strength of salvation: the fear of the LORD is his treasure.

The way I think about this verse is: "Here is something you can count on to be true for your entire life – CHoKMaH / Sophia (Wisdom) and DaTH (Divine Law, Spiritual Knowledge) are treasures that will be your YeSHuWaH (Jesus, salvation). The greatest treasure comes from uniting with God." Here we find two Kabbalah terms, Mother Wisdom, and a hidden reference to Jesus all within one verse.

The irrevocability of the DaTH (Divine Law) from God was not questioned by Jesus. Jesus was not out to destroy the ToWRaH representing the DaTH from God, but to bring it to life in the hearts of people. He was not getting out a giant cosmic eraser. What he challenged was that God's DaTH was complete and contained in scriptures and traditions. He offered that God's DaTH can be known in the heart, directly experienced, with continued insights into this DaTH, renewed revelation, and ongoing prophecy. This was not anti-Jewish at all. The idea was found in the Dead Sea Scrolls. The Jews continued to redefine DaTH with the Mishnah, the Talmud, the Kabbalah, and to this day with books being published, web sites being built, deeper insights explored and lived out.

Dialogue of the Saviour 30 Everyone who has known himself has seen goodness in everything given him to do.

Gnosis brings the state of wanting to act and respond in a good way. It becomes second nature to act out of compassion, out of empathy, out of good will.

Not to Destroy but To Fulfil

Matthew 5.17 Think not that I am come to destroy the law, or the prophets: I am not come to destroy, but to fulfil.

Matthew 5.18 For verily I say unto you, Till heaven and earth pass, one jot or one tittle shall in no wise pass from the law, till all be fulfilled.

"Jot" is used to translate iota, the smallest of the Greek alphabet letters. "Tittle" is an apostrophe mark, an accent mark. The "jot" and "tittle" were the smallest symbols in use in the printing presses that printed the Bible. The attempt was to translate the meaning into the modern context of 1607. Unfortunately the modernized concept is now antiquated. Perhaps today it should be: not the smallest letter, not the smallest punctuation mark, will pass from the law.

Matthew 5.19 Whosoever therefore shall break one of these least commandments, and shall teach men so, he shall be called the least in the kingdom of heaven: but whosoever shall do and teach them, the same shall be called great in the kingdom of heaven.

You have to beat them at their own game. Show them how it's done. Not be fake or false or a hypocrite. Discover the original heart and meaning behind the ancient concepts of how to be, and live it out in a way beyond merely reciting the words or representing the tradition. Find a living spiritual expression of sacredness. Every spiritual tradition has its unique rules. To honor one's traditional values is to connect to the life inherited and expected. Doing this mindfully instead of as learned habits of thoughts is empowering, not limiting; freeing, not confining.

Matthew 5.20 For I say unto you, That except your righteousness shall exceed the righteousness of the scribes and Pharisees, ye shall in no case enter into the kingdom of heaven.

By scribes, think "Bible-thumpers", those who think they have it all figured out by memorizing so many words and agreed upon interpretations. By Pharisee, think "Fundamentalists", those who see themselves as the only true representatives of their religion. You have to see beyond the literal readings, beyond the organized religion.

Apollonius of Tyana: Letter 43: To those who think themselves wise: If anyone claims to be my pupil, let him also claim that he remains

40

indoors, avoids all bathing, does not kill animals or eat their flesh, is free from envy, malignity, hatred, scandalmongering, and hostility, and is considered to belong to the class of free men.

Every spiritual tradition comes with expectations of what to do and what to avoid doing.

Didache 4.12-14 Thou shalt hate all hypocrisy, and everything that is not pleasing to the Lord. Thou shalt not forsake the commandments of the Lord, but thou shalt keep what thou didst receive, "adding nothing to it and taking nothing away." In the congregation thou shalt confess thy transgressions, and thou shalt not betake thyself to prayer with an evil conscience. This is the Way of Life.

Didache 6.1 See "that no one make thee to err" from this Way of the teaching, for he teaches thee without God.

Mark 10.18-19 And Jesus said unto him, Why callest thou me good? there is none good but one, that is, God. Thou knowest the commandments, Do not commit adultery, Do not kill, Do not steal, Do not bear false witness, Defraud not, Honour thy father and mother.

This "Law" fulfillment is core values to early Christianity, as is evident in these verses in Mark.

Lotus Sutra 14 When he opens his mouth to expound or when he reads the sutra, he should not delight in speaking of the faults of other people or scriptures. He should not display contempt for other teachers of the Law or speak of other people's tastes or shortcomings.

When you stand for what you know is real and authentic, there is no need to belittle other traditions. You can consider any way of thinking while faithfully representing your own core values. You can even discover how to express your core values in terms of their words and cherished quotations.

What if "Law" is more than the spiritual traditions of one specific culture? What if your "Law" is cosmopolitan?

AL MUMTAHINAH 60.12 O Prophet! When believing women come to thee to take the oath of fealty to thee, that they will not associate in worship any other thing whatever with Allah, that they will not steal, that they will not commit adultery (or fornication), that they will not kill their children, that they will not utter slander, intentionally forging falsehood, and that they will not disobey thee in any just matter – then do thou receive their fealty, and pray to Allah for the forgiveness (of their sins): for Allah is Oft-Forgiving, Most Merciful.

AL SAFF 61.6 And remember, Jesus, the son of Mary, said: "O Children of Israel! I am the messenger of Allah (sent) to you, confirming the Law (which came) before me, and giving Glad Tidings of a Messenger to come after me, whose name shall be Ahmad." But when he came to them with Clear Signs, they said, "This is evident sorcery!"

John 15.26 But when the Comforter is come, whom I will send unto you from the Father, even the Spirit of truth, which proceedeth from the Father, he shall testify of me:

Wouldn't it be unthinkable that God would only attempt to speak to humanity once and close the book forever? Jesus echoed the same truths that were spoken centuries before him, confirming them, explaining their heart, Muhammad explained. And in the same way, those who came centuries after Jesus with confirm his gospel, explain his heart. There is a timeline of voices, of those connected with and proceeding from the same Source.

YUNUS 10.37 This Qur'an is not such as can be produced by other than Allah; on the contrary it is a confirmation of (revelations) that went before it, and a fuller explanation of the Book – wherein there is no doubt – from the Lord of the worlds.

What other scriptures make the same claim? In how many languages and cultures did Allah attempt to reach the hearts of humanity? How many completely lost to us now? If the Qur'an is a confirmation of Allah having revealed the same truths to the many traditions and cultures and ages, then it has to in this confirmation-process admit to the inspirations found in this myriad of traditions. Beyond the distortions and corruptions of the tradition, there is a core of Truth to each of the many spiritual statements and traditions of the history of humanity. People back then could connect to "What is Real" and understand deeper truths and express them in their own languages and idioms. To seek the treasures from these traditions, we have to overlook what we cannot resonate with and cherry pick what speaks to us as significant and practical in our lives today. The thorns can be dismissed in the search for the beautiful and pleasantly scented roses.

AL A'RAF 7.196 "For my Protector is Allah, Who revealed the Book (from time to time), and He will choose and befriend the righteous.

AL 'IMRAN 3.3 It is He Who sent down to thee (step by step), in truth, the Book, confirming what went before it; and He sent down the Law (of Moses) and the Gospel (of Jesus) before this, as a guide to mankind, and He sent down the criterion (of judgment between right and wrong).

AL A'RAF 7.154 When the anger of Moses was appeased, he took up the tablets: in the writing thereon was guidance and Mercy for such as fear their Lord.

If you can see the value in the religion of your enemy, you are at a spiritually mature enough level to receive revelations that no one has ever before considered. Free your mind and open up yourself to however God wishes to speak to you.

Enmity of Enemies

Exodus 20.13 Thou shalt not kill.

Matthew 5.21 Ye have heard that it was said by them of old time, Thou shalt not kill; and whosoever shall kill shall be in danger of the judgment:

Matthew 5.22 But I say unto you, That whosoever is angry with his brother without a cause shall be in danger of the judgment: and whosoever shall say to his brother, Raca, shall be in danger of the council: but whosoever shall say, Thou fool, shall be in danger of hell fire.

Raca is an Aramaic word meaning empty-headed. Hell is Gehenna, meaning garbage dump. The word translated judgment is actually "crisis". This is one of those verses so full of meaning, but so lost in the translation. Consider this paraphrase: Going around mad with everyone all the time for what amounts to nothing is only creating crisis after crisis in your life. Keeping thinking you are the only one smart and everyone else is clueless will eventually place you in legal trouble. Thinking that everyone out there is a worthless moran will leave you being the one thrown on the trash heap of life.

Apollonius of Tyana: Letter 87: Apollonius to Aristocles: The passion of anger, if not tamed and cured, becomes a physical disease.

Apollonius of Tyana: Letter 88: Apollonius to Democrates: One who gets excessively angry over small wrongs prevents the offender from distinguishing his major faults from his minor ones.

AL NUR 24.19 Those who love (to see) scandal published broadcast among the Believers, will have a grievous Penalty in this life and in the Hereafter: Allah knows, and ye know not.

AL NUR 24.23 Those who slander chaste women, indiscreet but believing, are cursed in this life and in the Hereafter: for them is a grievous Penalty.

Pseudo-Phocylides 55-59 Do not afflict your heart with bygone evils; for what has been done can no more be undone. Do not be rash with your hands, but bridle your wild anger. For often someone who has dealt a blow has unintentionally committed a murder. Let your emotions be moderate, neither great nor overwhelming.

Sirach 28.1-4 He that revengeth shall find vengeance from the Lord, and he will surely keep his sins in remembrance. Forgive thy neighbour the hurt that he hath done unto thee, so shall thy sins also be forgiven when thou prayest. One man beareth hatred against another, and doth he seek pardon from the Lord? He sheweth no mercy to a man, which is like himself: and doth he ask forgiveness of his own sins?

Sirach 8.5 Reproach not a man that turneth from sin, but remember that we are all worthy of punishment.

Sirach is a text preserving the words of an ancient Jewish philosopher named Jesus, the son of Sirach. Early Christians would have had to have noticed this text, both for name and substance. It is included in Catholic Bibles but omitted from modern Protestant Bibles.

Didache 3.2 Be not proud, for pride leads to murder, nor jealous, nor contentious, nor passionate, for from all these murders are engendered.

Reconciliation of Brothers

Matthew 5.23 Therefore if thou bring thy gift to the altar, and there rememberest that thy brother hath ought against thee;

Matthew 5.24 Leave there thy gift before the altar, and go thy way; first be reconciled to thy brother, and then come and offer thy gift.

Apollonius of Tyana.1.11.2 The devout surely deserve good, your reverence, and the wicked the opposite. Hence, if the gods in their kindness find a man to be sincere and free from sin, they send him on his way crowned not with more crowns of gold, but with every blessing. But if they see a man to be besmirched and corrupt, they leave him to receive his retribution, showing their anger with him only insofar as he dared to enter a holy place when not in a state of purity.

Didache 14.1-3 On the Lord's Day of the Lord come together, break bread and hold Eucharist, after confessing your transgressions that your offering may be pure; but let none who has a quarrel with his fellow join in your meeting until they be reconciled, that your sacrifice be not defiled. For this is that which was spoken by the Lord, "In every place and time offer me a pure sacrifice, for I am a great king," saith the Lord, "and my name is wonderful among the heathen."

Didache 4.3-5 Thou shalt not desire a schism, but shalt reconcile those that strive. Thou shalt give righteous judgment; thou shalt favour no man's person in reproving transgression. Thou shalt not be of two minds whether it shall be or not. Be not one who stretches out his hands to receive, but shuts them when it comes to giving.

There is a sense of we are all one, and we are all made of divine stuff. In this light, if we only see the shortcomings of others, we stand judging the source of all, criticizing God manifest in individuality. If we see that we are all in it together, we can realize that when the other guy is stuck in frustration or whatever state, it could just as easily be ourselves in that same position. Peace takes priority over winning the argument.

Get Rid of your Adverse Nature

Matthew 5.25 Agree with thine adversary quickly, whiles thou art in the way with him; lest at any time the adversary deliver thee to the judge, and the judge deliver thee to the officer, and thou be cast into prison.

Matthew 5.26 Verily I say unto thee, Thou shalt by no means come out thence, till thou hast paid the uttermost farthing.

This is an interesting parable, one that is not usually taken for a parable. Who is the adversary? That would be Satan in Christian terms, Belial in ancient Jewish terms, Mara in Buddhist terms, Iblis in Islamic terms, the accuser, the great karmic accountant. What then is the prison? That would be the body, the trap for the spirit of light. The "cast into prison" is to incarnate. The "paid the uttermost farthing" is to balance out karmic debt. Of course, this interpretation does not agree with Paul based Christianity's justified by faith. Thus, most revert into taking this parable literally. The Pistis Sophia preserved the parable nature:

Pistis Sophia 113 If the soul goes out of the body and journeys on the way with the counterfeiting spirit, and if it has not found the mystery of releasing all the bonds and the seals which are bound to the counterfeiting spirit, so that it may stop being in charge of it, if then it has not found it, the counterfeiting spirit leads the soul to the Virgin of Light, the judge, and the judge, the Virgin of Light, examines the soul and discovers that it has sinned and not finding within it the mysteries of the Light, she delivers it to one of her receivers, and her receiver takes it and sends it into the body, and it does not emerge from the transformations of the body until it has completed its last circuit.

"Agree with thine adversary" then means to spank your inner monkey, to disconnect the mind game of your inner demons. Let go of anger and frustration and plotting revenge, and all those bad emotional states. Let it all go long before it consumes you and traps you.

Lust

Exodus 20.14 Thou shalt not commit adultery.

Matthew 5.27 Ye have heard that it was said by them of old time, Thou shalt not commit adultery:

Matthew 5.28 But I say unto you, That whosoever looketh on a woman to lust after her hath committed adultery with her already in his heart.

Matthew 5.29 And if thy right eye offend thee, pluck it out, and cast it from thee: for it is profitable for thee that one of thy members should perish, and not that thy whole body should be cast into hell.

Matthew 5.30 And if thy right hand offend thee, cut if off, and cast it from thee: for it is profitable for thee that one of thy members should perish, and not that thy whole body should be cast into hell.

Matthew 18.8-9 Wherefore if thy hand or thy foot offend thee, cut them off, and cast them from thee: it is better for thee to enter into life halt or maimed, rather than having two hands or two feet to be cast into everlasting fire. And if thine eye offend thee, pluck it out, and cast it from thee: it is better for thee to enter into life with one eye, rather than having two eyes to be cast into hell fire.

Matthew 18.8-9 is used in Matthew 5.29-30. You have to wonder if "eye" and "hand" really mean testicles. Better a castrated eunuch than a man who has sex with other men's wives, breaking up harmonious relationships and families.

Shepherd of Hermas Mandate 4 1.1-3 "I charge thee, "saith he, "to keep purity, and let not a thought enter into thy heart concerning another's wife, or concerning fornication, or concerning any such like evil deeds; for in so doing thou commitest a great sin. But remember thine own wife always, and thou shalt never go wrong. For should this desire enter into thine heart, thou wilt go wrong, and should any other as evil as this, thou commitest sin. For this desire in a servant of God is a great sin; and if any man doeth this evil deed, he worketh out death for himself. Look to it therefore. Abstain from this desire; for, where holiness dwelleth, there lawlessness ought not to enter into the heart of a righteous man."

Didache 3.3 My child, be not lustful, for lust leads to fornication, nor a speaker of base words, nor a lifter up of the eyes, for from all these is adultery engendered.

Apollonius of Tyana 1.13.3 Now Pythagoras was praised for saying that a man should not approach any woman except his wife, but according to Apollonius Pythagoras had prescribed that for others, but he himself was not going to marry or even have sexual intercourse. In this he surpassed the famous saying of Sophocles, who claimed that he had escaped from a raging, wild master when he reached old age. Thanks to his virtue and self-mastery, Apollonius was not subject to it even as an adolescent, but despite his youth and physical strength he overcame and "mastered" its rage.

Udanavarga 3.18 If one sees the danger of that which produces the suffering of craving, let one avoid that craving; without desire, without attachment, mindful, let the bhikkhu devote himself to the wandering life.

Proverbs 6.24-26 To keep thee from the evil woman, from the flattery of the tongue of a strange woman. Lust not after her beauty in thine heart; neither let her take thee with her eyelids. For by means of a whorish woman a man is brought to a piece of bread: and the adulteress will hunt for the precious life.

Vitakkasanthana Sutta 5 Just as a man with good eyes who did not want to see forms that he had come within range of sight would either shut his eyes or look away, so too if, while he is examining the danger in those thoughts, there still arise in him evil unwholesome thoughts connected with desire, with hate, and with delusion, then when a bhikkhu tries to forget those thoughts and does not give attention to them, then any evil unwholesome thoughts connected with desire, with hate, and with delusion are abandoned in him and subside. With the abandoning of them his mind becomes steadied internally, quieted, brought to singleness, and concentrated.

Alagaddupama Sutta 9 Bhikkus, that one can engage in sensual pleasures without sensual desires, without perceptions of sensual desire, without thoughts of sensual desire – that is impossible.

Salayatanasamyutta 132 For one with sense doors unguarded all the vows he undertakes are vain just like the wealth a man gains in a dream.

Bhagavad Gita 3.6 He who withdraws himself from actions, but ponders on their pleasures in his heart, he is under a delusion and is a false follower of the Path.

It is not enough what you do or don't do when the fields are strong and present. It is about what you say and don't say, what you want and don't want, and what you identify with and don't identify with. Stuff out there can consume you. Beware. Beyond law, there is a sense of higher values at play. It is not just about actions, it is in the realm of thoughts and feelings too. It's all in the mind.

AL NUR 24.31 And say to the believing women that they should lower their gaze and guard their modesty; that they should not display their beauty and ornaments except what (must ordinarily) appear thereof; that they should draw their veils over their bosoms and not display their beauty except to their husbands, their fathers, their husband's fathers, their sons, their husbands' sons, their brothers or their brothers' sons, or their sisters' sons, or their women, or the slaves whom their right hands possess, or male servants free of physical needs, or small children who have no sense of the shame of sex; and that they should not strike their feet in order to draw attention to their hidden ornaments. And O ye Believers! Turn ye all together towards Allah, that ye may attain Bliss.

Bhagavad Gita 16.12-16 They are bound by hundreds of vain hopes. Anger and lust is their refuge; and they strive by unjust means to amass wealth for their own cravings. 'I have gained this today, and I shall attain this desire. This wealth is mine, and that shall also be mine. I have slain that enemy, and others also slay. I am a lord, I enjoy life, I am successful, powerful and happy. I am wealthy and of noble birth: who else is there like me? I shall pay for religious rituals, I shall make benefactions, I shall enjoy myself.' Thus they say in their darkness of delusion. Led astray by many wrong thoughts, entangled in the net of delusion, enchained to the pleasures of their cravings, they fall down into a foul hell.

Sex is wrapped around competition, conquest, money, mind games, trickery, obligations, and possessiveness. Who has the prettiest trophy wife? Who has the richest husband?

When it's all about winning, victory, achieving, acquiring the tangible, then the tangible is all you get. Belly full. Job secure. Paycheck. Riding "the system" that the world has put into place. It is a trap. It is a delusion. It won't last and it takes away your lifetime from being able to focus on the gnosis that is real.

Svetasvatara Upanishad 2 The chariot of the mind is drawn by wild horses, and those wild horses have to be tamed.

Sanctity of Marriage

Deuteronomy 24.1-2 When a man hath taken a wife, and married her, and it come to pass that she find no favour in his eyes, because he hath found some uncleanness in her: then let him write her a bill of divorcement, and give it in her hand, and send her out of his house. And when she is departed out of his house, she may go and be another man's wife.

Matthew 5.31 It hath been said, Whosoever shall put away his wife, let him give her a writing of divorcement:

Matthew 5.32 But I say unto you, That whosoever shall put away his wife, saving for the cause of fornication, causeth her to commit adultery: and whosoever shall marry her that is divorced committeth adultery.

Bezae Cantabrigiensis and Italic manuscripts omit the last part of this verse: and whosoever shall marry her that is divorced committeth adultery.

Gasp. Jesus actually argues against a sacred verse of the Law of Moses, against the "men rule" tradition, against the thought that women are just property that can be owned or dismissed for any reason the man sees fit. Divorce not only breaks up families, it to this day puts recently married people "back on the market", it rips the vows of marriage as if they had never taken place. Once we agree to take someone in as family, agree to support them and encourage them, such an oath should be considered sacred to us.

AL NUR 24.3 Let no man guilty of adultery or fornication marry any but a woman similarly guilty, or an Unbeliever: nor let any but such a woman or an Unbeliever marry such a man: to the Believers such a thing is forbidden.

Matthew 19.3-9 is summarized in its use in Matthew 5.31-32.

Matthew 19.3-15 The Pharisees also came unto him, tempting him, and saying unto him, Is it lawful for a man to put away his wife for every cause? And he answered and said unto them, Have ye not read, that he which made them at the beginning made them male and female, and said, For this cause shall a man leave father and mother, and shall cleave to his wife: and they twain shall be one flesh? Wherefore they are no more twain, but one flesh. What therefore God hath joined together, let not man put asunder. They say unto him, Why did Moses then command to give a writing of divorcement, and to put her away? He saith unto them, Moses because of the hardness of your hearts suffered you to put away your wives: but from the beginning it was not so. And I say unto you, Whosoever shall put away his wife, except it be for fornication, and shall marry another, committeth adultery: and whoso marrieth her which is put away doth commit adultery. His disciples say unto him, If the case of the man be so with his wife, it is not good to marry. But he said unto them, All men cannot receive this saying, save they to whom it is given. For there are some eunuchs, which were so born from their mother's womb: and there are some eunuchs, which were made eunuchs of men: and there be eunuchs, which have made themselves eunuchs for the kingdom of heaven's sake. He that is able to receive it, let him receive it. Then were there brought unto him little children, that he should put his hands on them, and pray: and the disciples rebuked them. But Jesus said, Suffer little children, and forbid them not, to come unto me: for of such is the kingdom of heaven. And he laid his hands on them, and departed thence.

I wonder if the little children coming to be touched by Jesus were there to take vows of celibacy? There are traditions of holy orders initiating young people into becoming monks and nuns, with vows of celibacy and poverty, both in Christian tradition and in Buddhist tradition.

1 Corinthians 7.27 Art thou bound unto a wife? seek not to be loosed. Art thou loosed from a wife? seek not a wife.

Swearing / Vows

Leviticus 19.12 And ye shall not swear by my name falsely, neither shalt thou profane the name of thy God: I am the LORD.

Deuteronomy 23.23 That which is gone out of thy lips thou shalt keep and perform; even a freewill offering, according as thou hast vowed unto the LORD thy God, which thou hast promised with thy mouth.

Matthew 5.33 Again, ye have heard that it hath been said by them of old time, Thou shalt not forswear thyself, but shalt perform unto the Lord thine oaths:

Matthew 5.34 But I say unto you, Swear not at all; neither by heaven; for it is God's throne:

Matthew 5.35 Nor by the earth; for it is his footstool: neither by Jerusalem; for it is the city of the great King.

Matthew 5.36 Neither shalt thou swear by thy head, because thou canst not make one hair white or black.

Even your own head does not belong to you. You can't concentrate and focus your will strongly enough to cause one white hair to grow, much less one black hair. Your city, your planet, your cosmos, none of these rise and set in your armpits. None of these respond to your summoning, to your invoking. You are just not that magical.

Didache 3.4 My child, regard not omens, for this leads to idolatry; neither be an enchanter, nor an astrologer, nor a magician, neither wish to see these things, for from them all is idolatry engendered.

Sirach 23.8-9 The sinner shall be left in his foolishness: both the evil speaker and the proud shall fall thereby. Accustom not thy mouth to swearing; neither use thyself to the naming of the Holy One.

I am ashamed of Christianity when I hear that someone has set a date for Jesus to return, or for the world to end. They have all been wrong. They have been wrong on so many levels at the same time. And yet, to many, they define Christianity to the world around them.

Simple Words

Matthew 5.37 But let your communication be, Yea, yea; Nay, nay: for whatsoever is more than these cometh of evil.

LUQMAN 31.19 "And be moderate in thy pace, and lower thy voice; for the harshest of sounds without doubt is the braying of the ass."

James 3.2 Anyone who does not trip up in speech has reached perfection and is able to keep the body on a tight rein.

Pseudo-Phocylides 50 Be sincere to all, speak what is from your soul.

Apollonius of Tyana: Letter 92: Apollonius to his pupils: Take great care not to say what you should not. For it is the absolute mark of an uncultured person not to be able to stay silent and to blurt out improprieties.

Apollonius of Tyana: Letter 93: Apollonius to his pupils: Talkativeness causes many a mistake, but silence is safe.

Apollonius of Tyana: Letter 94: Apollonius to Euphrates: The best people use the fewest words. That is why, if chatterers felt as much annoyance as they cause, they would not make long speeches.

Apollonius of Tyana 1.14.2 He says that this way of life, which he practices for five whole years, was extremely difficult. He could not speak when he had much to say, and could not hear when he heard much to make him angry. He was impelled to correct many people, but said to himself, "Bear up, my heart, and my tongue too." And when remarks offended him he deferred refuting them for a time.

A vow of silence was an important part of the spirituality of Pythagoras, was practiced in ancient times by Buddhists and Hindus, and became an integral part of several of the Christian monastic orders.

Saccasamyutta 10 Bhikkus, do not engage in the various kinds of pointless talk, that is, talk about kings, thieves, and ministers of state; talk about armies, dangers, and wars; talk about food, drink, garments, and beds; talk about garlands and scents; talk about relations, vehicles, villages, towns, cities, and countries; talk about women and talk about heroes; street talk and talk by the well; talk about those departed in days gone by; rambling chitchat; speculation about the world and about the sea; talk about becoming this or that.

Devatasamyutta 61 Name [words, labels] has weighed down everything; nothing is more extensive than name. Name is the one thing that has all under its control.

Udanavarga 8.2 When a man is born, an axe grows in his mouth; he cuts himself with that axe when using wrong speech.

Kena Upanishad 2 He comes to the thought of those who know him beyond thought, not to those who imagine he can be attained by thought. He is unknown to the learned and known to the simple.

Beyond words, beyond logic, just knowing, the real secret is simple, yet very profound. Preachers with lots of words in long drawn out boring sermons have missed the point. Keep it simple. Keep it practical. Keep it short. Keep it real.

Tao Te Ching 56 Those who know do not talk. Those who talk do not know. Keep your mouth closed.

Revenge and Peaceful Response

You can see the evolution of Judaism here. Even the Exodus verse is a great compassionate leap from the practice of revenge literally being overkill for the wrong inflicted.

Exodus 21.23-25 And if any mischief follow, then thou shalt give life for life, Eye for eye, tooth for tooth, hand for hand, foot for foot, Burning for burning, wound for wound, stripe for stripe.

AL MA'IDAH 5.45 We ordained therein for them: "Life for life, eye for eye, nose for nose, ear for ear, tooth for tooth, and wounds equal for equal." But if any one remits the retaliation by way of charity, it is an act of atonement for himself. And if any fail to judge by (the light of) what Allah hath revealed, they are (No better than) wrong-doers.

AL HUJURAT 49.9 If two parties among the Believers fall into a quarrel, make ye peace between them: but if one of them transgresses beyond bounds against the other, then fight ye (all) against the one that transgresses until it complies with the command of Allah; but if it complies, then make peace between them with justice, and be fair: for Allah loves those who are fair (and just).

Psalm 37.8 Cease from anger, and forsake wrath: fret not thyself in any wise to do evil.

Dead Sea Scrolls Community Rule 1QS 10.17-19 When distress breaks out I shall praise Him, and in His salvation shall I rejoice. To no man shall I return evil for evil, I shall pursue a man only for good; for with God resides the judgment of all the living, and He shall pay each man his recompense. My zeal shall not be tarnished by a spirit of wickedness, neither shall I lust for riches gained through violence.

Pseudo-Phocylides 142-144 It is better to make a gracious friend instead of an enemy. Nip the evil in the bud, and heal the wound. By a tiny spark a vast forest is set on fire.

Pseudo-Phocylides 77-78 Do not imitate evil, but leave vengeance to justice. For persuasiveness is a blessing, but strife begets only strife.

Eye for an Eye

Matthew 5.38 Ye have heard that it hath been said, An eye for an eye, and a tooth for a tooth:

Matthew 5.39 But I say unto you, That ye resist not evil: but whosoever shall smite thee on thy right cheek, turn to him the other also.

Matthew 5.40 And if any man will sue thee at the law, and take away thy coat, let him have thy cloak also.

Matthew 5.41 And whosoever shall compel thee to go a mile, go with him twain.

Shepherd of Hermas Mandate 5 1.1-3 "Be thou long-suffering and understanding," he saith, "and thou shalt have the mastery over all evil deeds, and shalt work all righteousness. For if thou art long-suffering, the Holy Spirit that abideth in thee shall be pure, not being darkened by another evil spirit, but dwelling in a large room shall rejoice and be glad with the vessel in which he dwelleth, and shall serve God with much cheerfulness, having prosperity in himself. But if any angry temper approach, forthwith the Holy Spirit, being delicate, is straitened, not having the place clear, and seeketh to retire from the place; for he is being choked by the evil spirit, and has no room to minister unto the Lord, as he desireth, being polluted by angry temper. For the Lord dwelleth in long-suffering, but the devil in angry temper.

There is an old Southern phrase, "losing my religion", which means to lose your temper. Maintain the spirit at all costs. Then they can hit you and take from you and push you around, but they can't break your spirit. If your religion is your calm cool headed easy going true nature, it is important to maintain this state as much as possible.

Shepherd of Hermas Mandate 5 2.4-7 But angry temper is in the first place foolish, fickle and senseless; then from foolishness is engendered bitterness, and from bitterness wrath, and from wrath anger, and from anger spite; then spite being composed of all these evil elements becometh a great sin and incurable. For when all these spirits dwell in one vessel, where the Holy Spirit also dwelleth, that vessel cannot contain them, but overfloweth. The delicate spirit therefore, as not being accustomed to dwell with an evil spirit nor with harshness, departeth from a man of that kind, and seeketh to dwell with gentleness and tranquility. Then, when it hath removed from that man, in whom it dwells, that man becometh emptied of the righteous spirit, and henceforward, being filled with the evil spirits, he is unstable in all his actions, being dragged about hither and thither by the evil spirits, and is altogether blinded and bereft of his good intent. Thus then it happeneth to all persons of angry temper.

1 Peter 3.9 Not rendering evil for evil, or railing for railing: but contrariwise blessing; knowing that ye are thereunto called, that ye should inherit a blessing.

Udanavarga 8.9 Even if a wrong word is uttered, one should not utter one in reply; he who utters a similar one is enslaved; the wise do not answer thus; wrong words are uttered only by the foolish.

Udanavarga 9.12-13 If, when committing bad actions, the fool does not become aware of what he does, the stupid man is burned by his own actions as if by fire. The foolish, whose wisdom is false, behave towards each other as towards enemies, committing bad action which is a fruit filled with bitterness.

It is bad if it initiates out of the blue, but it is also bad if arisen as a knee-jerk response. It doesn't matter who started it, it matters how you engage in it.

Didache 1.4 "Abstain from carnal" and bodily "lusts." "If any man smite thee on the right cheek, turn to him the other cheek also," and thou wilt be perfect. "If any man impress thee to go with him one mile, go with him two. If any man take thy coat, give him thy shirt also. If any man will take from thee what is thine, refuse it not" – not even if thou canst.

Matthew 18.21-22 Then came Peter to him, and said, Lord, how oft shall my brother sin against me, and I forgive him? till seven times? Jesus saith unto him, I say not unto thee, Until seven times: but, Until seventy times seven.

Matthew 26.52 Put away your sword. All who use a sword will die by a sword.

Lamentations 3.25-30 The LORD is good unto them that wait for him, to the soul that seeketh him. It is good that a man should both hope and quietly wait for the salvation of the LORD. It is good for a man that he bear the yoke in his youth. He sitteth alone and keepeth silence, because he hath borne it upon him. He putteth his mouth in the dust; if so be there may be hope. He giveth his cheek to him that smiteth him: he is filled full with reproach.

Mahadukkhakklandha Sutta 12 Men take swords and shields and buckle on bows and quivers, and they charge into battle massed in double array with arrows and spears flying and swords flashing; and there they are wounded by arrows and spears, and their heads are cut off by swords, whereby they incur death or deadly suffering.

Kosalasamyutta 15 The killer begets a killer, one who conquers, a conqueror. The abuser begets abuse, the reviler, one who reviles. Thus by the unfolding of karma the plunderer is plundered.

Kakacupama Sutta 6 My mind will be unaffected, and I shall utter no evil words; I shall abide compassionate for his welfare, with a mind of loving-kindness, without inner hate. If anyone should give you a blow with his hand, with a clod, with a stick, or with a knife, you should abandon any desires and any thoughts based on the household life.

Kakacupama Sutta 20 Bhikkhus, even if bandits were to sever you savagely limb by limb with a two-handed saw, he who gave rise to a mind of hate towards them would not be carrying out my teaching.

Dhammapada 17.3 Overcome anger by peacefulness: overcome evil with good. Overcome the mean by generosity; and the man who lies with truth.

Tao Te Ching 63 Reward bitterness with care.

Brahmanasamyutta 2, Sakkasamyutta 4 How can anger arise in one who is angerless, in the tamed one of righteous living, in one liberated by perfect knowledge, in the Stable One who abides in peace? One who repays an angry man with anger thereby makes things worse for himself. Not repaying an angry man with anger, one wins a battle hard to win. He practices for the welfare of both – his own and the other's – when, knowing that his foe is angry, he mindfully maintains his peace.

AL ANFAL 8.61 But if the enemy incline towards peace, do thou (also) incline towards peace, and trust in Allah: for He is One that heareth and knoweth (all things).

AL SHURA 42.39-40 And those who, when an oppressive wrong is inflicted on them, (are not cowed but) help and defend themselves. The recompense for an injury is an injury equal thereto (in degree): but if a person forgives and makes reconciliation, his reward is due from Allah: for (Allah) loveth not those who do wrong.

AL SHURA 42.43 But indeed if any show patience and forgive, that would truly be an exercise of courageous will and resolution in the conduct of affairs.

Abu 'Abdallah Ahmad b. Muhammad al-Shaybani Ibn Hanbal: Kitab al-Zuhd 481 Jesus was walking by the Pass of Afiq with one of his disciples. A man crossed their path and prevented them from proceeding, saying, "I will not let you pass until I have struck each of you a blow." They tried to dissuade him but he refused. Jesus said, "Here is my cheek. Slap it." The map slapped it and let him pass. He then said to the disciple, "I will not let you pass until I have slapped you too." The disciple refused. When Jesus saw this, he offered him his other cheek. He slapped it and allowed both to go. Jesus then said, "O God, if this is pleasing to You, your pleasure has reached me. If it does not please You, You are more worthy of righteous anger."

Become a Provider of Giving

Didache 1.5-6 Give to everyone that asks thee, and do not refuse, for the Father's will is that we give to all from the gifts we have received. Blessed is he that gives according to the mandate; for he is innocent. Woe to him who receives; for if any man receive alms under pressure of need he is innocent; but he who receives it without need shall be tried as to why he took and for what, and being in prison he shall be examined as to his deeds, and "he shall not come out thence until he pay the last farthing." But concerning this it was also said, "Let thine alms sweat into thine hands until thou knowest to whom thou art giving."

Matthew 5.42 Give to him that asketh thee, and from him that would borrow of thee turn not thou away.

This verse seems to be supplied as a way of thinking to be surpassed. Give to everyone who asks and let God sort it out instead of figuring out who is truly needy and who is being deceitful in asking for a handout.

Psalm 37.21 The wicked borroweth, and payeth not again: but the righteous sheweth mercy, and giveth.

Some folks are only looking out for themselves. Some folks are looking for opportunities to help others. It is the difference between those who look for opportunities to take advantage of those gullible enough to trust them and those who look for opportunities to help everyone, even those who are trying to take advantage of their charity.

Yakkhasamyutta 12 Doing what is proper, dutiful, one with initiative finds wealth. By truthfulness one wins acclaim; giving, one binds friends. That is how one does not sorrow when passing from this world to the next.

Deuteronomy 15.7-8 If there be among you a poor man of one of thy brethren within any of thy gates in thy land which the LORD thy God giveth thee, thou shalt not harden thine heart, nor shut thine hand from thy poor brother: But thou shalt open thine hand wide unto him, and shalt surely lend him sufficient for his need, in that which he wanteth.

Deuteronomy 15.10-11 Thou shalt surely give him, and thine heart shall not be grieved when thou givest unto him: because that for this thing the LORD thy God shall bless thee in all thy works, and in all that thou puttest thine hand unto. For the poor shall never cease out of the land: therefore I command thee, saying, Thou shalt open thine hand wide unto thy brother, to thy poor, and to thy needy, in thy land.

Shepherd of Hermas Mandate 2 1.4 But clothe thyself in reverence, wherein is no evil stumbling-block, but all things are smooth and gladsome. Work that which is good, and of thy labors, which God giveth thee, give to all that are in want freely, not questioning to whom thou shalt give, and to whom thou shalt not give. Give to all; for to all God desireth that there should be given of His own bounties.

Tobit 4.7-11 Give alms of thy substance; and when thou givest alms, let not thine eye be envious, neither turn thy face from any poor, and the face of God shall not be turned away from thee. If thou hast abundance give alms accordingly: if thou have but a little, be not afraid to give according to that little: For thou layest up a good treasure for thyself against the day of necessity. Because that alms do deliver from death, and suffereth not to come into darkness. For alms is a good gift unto all that give it in the sight of the most High.

Mahavagga 8.26.3 Monks, you have no mother, you have no father, who might tend to you. If you don't tend to one another, who then will tend to you? Whoever would tend to me, should tend to the sick.

Sotapattisamyutta 6 He dwells at home with a mind devoid of the stain of stinginess, freely generous, open-handed, delighting in relinquishment, one devoted to charity, delighting in giving and sharing.

AL BAQARAH 2.280 If the debtor is in a difficulty, grant him time till it is easy for him to repay. But if ye remit it by way of charity, that is best for you if ye only knew.

Cut them some slack. Cut them lots of slack. What if it were the other way around? Wouldn't you hope that they'd give you a break?

Friend and Enemy

Jubilees 20.2a And he commanded them that they should guard the way of the Lord so that they might do righteousness and each one might love his neighbor.

Matthew 5.43 Ye have heard that it hath been said, Thou shalt love thy neighbour, and hate thine enemy.

Dead Sea Scrolls Community Rule 1QS 1.9-11 He is to teach them both to love all the Children of Light – each commensurate with his rightful place in the council of God – and to hate all the Children of Darkness, each commensurate with his guilt and the vengeance due him from God.

The distinction between neighbor and enemy, good and evil, light and darkness, was carried out to its practical conclusion of exercising love for the neighbor and hatred for the enemy. It is this mindset that Jesus is questioning here.

John 15.12 This is my commandment, That ye love one another, as I have loved you.

John 13.34-35 A new commandment I give unto you, That ye love one another; as I have loved you, that ye also love one another. By this shall all men know that ye are my disciples, if ye have love one to another.

1 John 4.7-8 My dear friends, let us love one another, since love is from God and everyone who loves is a child of God and knows God. He that loveth not knoweth not God; for God is love.

1 John 2.10 He that loveth his brother abideth in the light, and there is none occasion of stumbling in him.

Leviticus 19.17-18 Thou shalt not hate thy brother in thine heart: thou shalt in any wise rebuke thy neighbour, and not suffer sin upon him. Thou shalt not avenge, nor bear any grudge against the children of thy people, but thou shalt love thy neighbour as thyself: I am the LORD.

Deuteronomy 10.19 Love ye therefore the stranger: for ye were strangers in the land of Egypt.

Jesus actually corrects a misconception about the Law promoting xenophobia. He reminds us that the Law also promotes love for foreigners.

Psalm 109.28 Let them curse, but bless thou: when they arise, let them be ashamed; but let thy servant rejoice.

Thomas 25 Jesus said, "Love your brother like your soul, guard him like the pupil of your eye."

We may question who "brothers" are in the mind of Jesus. Who is "us" that is not one of "them"? Jesus challenged the idea that Christ belongs just to the descendants of David the king (Matthew 22.42), and that the chosen people are limited to the descendants of Abraham (Matthew 3.9). He was descendant of Adam, "son of man", "child of humanity", and it is to this global extreme that he extends his definition of friends, of the family of man, the descendants of Adam.

Bhagavad Gita 6.9 He has risen on the heights of his soul. And in peace he beholds relatives, companions and friends, those impartial or indifferent or who hate him: he sees them all with the same inner peace.

Bhagavad Gita 12.18-19 The man whose love is the same for his enemies, or his friends, whose soul is the same in honour or disgrace, who is beyond heat or cold or pleasure or pain, who is free from the chains of attachments; who is balanced in blame and in praise, whose soul is silent, who is happy with whatever he has, whose home is not in this world, and who has love – this man is dear to me.

Bhagavad Gita 14.24-25 Who dwells in his inner self, and is the same in pleasure and pain; to whom gold or stones or earth are one, and what is pleasing or displeasing leave him in peace; who is beyond both praise and blame, and whose mind is steady and quiet; Who is the same in honour or disgrace, and has the same love for enemies or friends, who surrenders all selfish undertakings – this man has gone beyond the three.

This is the common focal pattern, the main idea, the summation of the resonance between Krishna and Buddha and Christ: Don't just love those who you like, extend the definition of family outward until it includes those who you don't know and even those who you don't like. If, on a global basis, we all helped a little more than we need to be helped, gave more than we get, cared more than we need to be cared for, then the overall balance of the human equation would mean that everyone is helped, everyone is fed, everyone is OK, no one is left out of the human family. It should not be about which religion wins, but which ideals win.

FUSSILAT 41.34 Nor can goodness and Evil be equal. Repel (Evil) with what is better: Then will he between whom and thee was hatred become as it were thy friend and intimate!

Good overpowers evil. Right wins out over wrong. It is not just in comic books. If it is exercised, good always wins in the end. Change for the better eventually comes.

AL MUMTAHINAH 60.7 It may be that Allah will grant love (and friendship) between you and those whom ye (now) hold as enemies. For Allah has power (over all things); And Allah is Oft-Forgiving, Most Merciful.

I love it that these quotes are Islamic. Love overcomes hatred. Brotherhood of man overcomes xenophobia. Reach out with compassion to those radically different from you and embrace them. Give them a forgiving, merciful hug.

Dhammapada 1.5 For hate is not conquered by hate: hate is conquered by love. This is a law eternal.

Upakkilesa Sutta 6 'He abused me, he struck me, he defeated me, he robbed me' – in those who harbor thoughts like these hatred will never be allayed. For in this world hatred is never allayed by further acts of hate. It is allayed by non-hatred: that is the fixed and ageless law. Those others do not recognize that here we should restrain ourselves. But those wise ones who realize this at once end all their enmity.

Love

Matthew 5.44 But I say unto you, Love your enemies, bless them that curse you, do good to them that hate you, and pray for them which despitefully use you, and persecute you;

Kakacupama Sutta 11 Our minds will remain unaffected, and we shall utter no evil words; we shall abide compassionate for their welfare, with a mind of loving-kindness, without inner hate. We shall abide pervading that person with a mind imbued with loving-kindness, and starting with him, we shall abide pervading the all-encompassing world with a mind imbued with loving-kindness, abundant, exalted, immeasurable, without hostility and without ill will.

Bojjhangasamyutta 51 There is, bhikkhus, the liberation of mind through lovingkindness: frequently giving careful attention to it is the denourishment that prevents unarisen ill will from arising, and arisen ill will from increasing and expanding.

Love de-nourishes hate, starves it, poisons it, kills it off.

Kosalasamyutta 8 Having traversed all quarters with the mind, one finds none anywhere dearer than oneself. Likewise, each person holds himself most dear; hence one who loves himself should not harm others.

Put "you" in the place of everyone you encounter and you will change the way you react to them.

Dhammapada 15.1-3 O let us live in joy, in love amongst those who hate! Among men who hate, let us live in love. O let us live in joy, in health amongst those who are ill! Among men who are ill, let us live in health. O let us live in joy, in peace amongst those who struggle! Among men who struggle, let us live in peace. O let us live in joy, although having nothing! In joy let us live like spirits of light!

Cittasamyutta 7, Vatthupama Sutta 16 Thus above, below, across, and everywhere, and to all as to himself, he dwells pervading the entire world with a mind imbued with lovingkindness, vast, exalted, measureless, without hostility, without ill will.

Tevijja Sutta 76-77 Thus he dwells suffusing the whole world, upwards, downwards, across, everywhere, always with a heart filled with loving-kindness, abundant, unbounded, without hate or ill-will. Just as if a mighty trumpeter were with little difficulty to make a proclamation to the four quarters, so by this meditation, Vasettha, by this liberation of the heart through loving-kindness he leaves nothing untouched, nothing unaffected in the sensuous sphere. This, Vasettha, is the way to union with Brahma (God).

Blow a trumpet as loud as you can and consider that is the same as saying "I love you" to everyone close enough to hear your music. Namaste

Brahma is love. Buddha concluded this five hundred years before the dawn of the Christian age, three thousand miles from Israel, teaching in terms of the Hindu religion of the people around him. I think no matter what age and in what culture Buddha had have lived, his message would have been the same. Zeus is love. Allah is compassion. Yahweh is CHeSeD. Beyond the dogmatic assertions and mind games of religion, to reach the true mystical heart of whatever tradition you have found yourself in, open up your heart to loving-kindness, to empathy, to compassion, to love, and by gnosis of this you will have connected to your Beloved. God truly is love. Buddha teaches how to unite with God. Beyond dogmatic mind games, the bottom line is very simple and profound. God is love. Awakening is love. Enlightenment is love. Find one and you've found them all.

Abu 'Abdallah Ahmad b. Muhammad al-Shaybani Ibn Hanbal: Kitab al-Zuhd 317 Jesus used to say, "Charity does not mean doing good to him who does good to you, for this is to return good for good. Charity means that you should do good to him who does you harm."

Abu 'Abdallah Ahmad b. Muhammad al-Shaybani Ibn Hanbal: Kitab al-Zuhd 480 Christ said, "If you desire to devote yourselves entirely to God and to be the light of the children of Adam, forgive those who have done you evil, visit the sick who do not visit you, be kind to those who are unkind to you, and lend to those who do not repay you."

Abu 'Uthman 'Amr b. Bahr Al-Jahiz: Al-Bayan wa al-Tabyin 2.177 Christ passed by a group of Israelites who insulted him. Every time they spoke a word of evil, Christ answered with good. Simon the pure said to him, "Will you answer them with good each time they speak evil?" Christ said, "Each person spends of what he owns."

What if we all own God and share God and represent God? We collect God like a miser collects money? We consume God like a glutton eating a buffet? What if love becomes our energy source, our obsession? We bring into our surrounding worlds the effects of love and peace and forgiveness and empathy, solutions and dreams for a better world? What if we thought of "God" as not being a noun, but instead thought of "God" as being a verb? What if "I God you" would mean the same as "I love you"?

All Inclusive

Matthew 5.45 That ye may be the children of your Father which is in heaven: for he maketh his sun to rise on the evil and on the good, and sendeth rain on the just and on the unjust.

Apollonius of Tyana: Letter 44.2: To Hestiaeus, his brother: And yet you are well aware that it is an honorable thing to regard the whole earth as one's ancestral city, and all humans as his brothers and friends, since we are all akin to God, have a single nature, and have the same community of thought and emotions with[in] each and every person, wherever and however we may have come into existence, whether barbarian or Greek, so long as we are human.

AL SHURA 42.28 He is the One that sends down rain (even) after (men) have given up all hope, and scatters His Mercy (far and wide). And He is the Protector, Worthy of all Praise.

QAF 50.9 And We send down from the sky rain charted with blessing, and We produce therewith Gardens and Grain for harvests;

AL NAHL 16.65 And Allah sends down rain from the skies, and gives therewith life to the earth after its death: verily in this is a Sign for those who listen.

Lotus Sutra 5 I appear in the world like a great cloud that showers moisture upon all the dry and withered living beings, so that all are able to escape suffering, gain the joy of peace and security, the joys of this world and the joys of nirvana. [...] I bring fullness and satisfaction to the world, like a rain that spreads its moisture everywhere. Eminent and lowly, superior and inferior, observers of precepts, violators of precepts, those fully endowed with proper demeanor, those not fully endowed, those of correct views, of erroneous views, of keen capacity, of dull capacity – I cause the Dharma rain to rain on all equally, never lax or neglectful.

Dharma rain. Gospel rain. Same wetness.

Bhagavad Gita 13.33 And even as one sun gives light to all things in this world, so the Lord of the field gives light to all his field.

Tables turned. Last becomes first. Stuff that used to stop you doesn't matter anymore. Stuff that used to be unappreciated, even disdained, is now become fashion. Love shifts values and priorities. Devotion shifts how the devotees are thought of. Stuff that used to divide good from evil now no longer matters. It is like sunshine or rain or wind not caring about who receives how much. What used to matter is now unimportant. The flood doesn't care how much things are valued. Everyone is given an even shot at it. The overly religious fanatics don't have the first of the line anymore. Those who "get it" are placed first, even if they are the most unlikely to have ever gotten anything spiritual at all. They are brought to the first of the line because they are awakened enough to respond to the event at hand.

Beyond Ordinary

Matthew 5.46 For if ye love them which love you, what reward have ye? do not even the publicans the same?

Matthew 5.47 And if ye salute your brethren only, what do ye more than others? do not even the publicans so?

Publicans could be thought of as "corrupt politicians" and the meaning becomes clear.

Thomas 95 Jesus said, "If you have money, do not lend it at interest, but give it to one from whom you will not get it back."

Didache 1.3 Now, the teaching of these words is this: "Bless those that curse you, and pray for your enemies, and fast for those that persecute you. For what credit is it to you if you love those that love you? Do not even the heathen do the same?" But, for your part, "love those that hate you," and you will have no enemy.

Tao Te Ching 49 I am good to people who are good. I am also good to people who are not good. Because virtue is goodness. I have faith in people who are faithful. I also have faith in people who are not faithful. Because virtue is faithfulness.

Metta Sutta 7 Even as a mother, as long as she doth live, watches over her child, her only child, even so should one practise an all-embracing mind unto all beings.

What if everyone out there was welcomed and loved in the same way we welcome home our own child who has been away?

Perfect

Matthew 5.48 Be ye therefore perfect, even as your Father which is in heaven is perfect.

Shepherd of Hermas Mandate 12 6.1-3 "But I, the angel of repentance, say unto you; Fear not the devil; for I was sent," saith he, "to be with you who repent with your whole heart, and to strengthen you in the faith. Believe, therefore, on God, ye who by reason of your sins have despaired of your life, and are adding to your sins, and weighing down your life; for if ye turn unto the Lord with your whole heart, and work righteousness the remaining days of your life, and serve Him rightly according to His will, He will give healing to your former sins, and ye shall have power to master the works of the devil. But of the threatening of the devil fear not at all; for he is unstrung, like the sinews of a dead man. Hear me therefore, and fear Him, Who is able to do all things, to save and to destroy, and observe these commandments, and ye shall live unto God."

Don't think there is some evil force out there too powerful. You weighed yourself down and you can let go of whatever it is that prevents you from that light synergy connection to God. And once connected, perfection is the one and only option. Imperfections are just distractions from your natural state.

The concept of working out your salvation, striving for perfection, is lost in modern Christianity that just wants you to know you've been "saved". The quest for sanctification needs desperately to be reintroduced into modern Christianity.

Didache 6.2 For if thou canst bear the whole yoke of the Lord, thou wilt be perfect, but if thou canst not, do what thou canst.

Corpus Hermeticum 12.20 God is both around all and through all, he is activity and power, and so to experience God's presence is not difficult, my son.

John 17.22-23 And the glory which thou gavest me I have given them; that they may be one, even as we are one: I in them, and thou in me, that they may be made perfect in one; and that the world may know that thou hast sent me, and hast loved them, as thou hast loved me.

Desiring perfection is short-circuited by "faith without works" religion, by the un-moveable weight of "original sin" and the "can't do anything but have faith and trust in Jesus" mindset. John Wesley, the founder of the Methodist Church, realized that beyond the salvation of justification, Christians should be striving for the sanctification that comes with the uniting with the Holy Ghost. It is from the perspective of this mystical quest that the same personal transformation goals can be recognized in various other spiritual traditions.

The bottom line is not agreeing to believe in stuff, but rather, it is agreeing to participate in personal transformation, regaining of personal integrity. The vision must seep through intentions, through words, through actions, through interactions, through contributions, through participation, through identification.

Udanavarga 4.5-6 Through endeavor, through heedfulness, through chastity, through self-mastery, the sensible man creates an island where the waves cannot overwhelm him. Whoever practices endeavor, mindfulness, upright thought, considered action, chastity, living within the Doctrine, the heedful one such as this ever increases in glory.

Udanavarga 10.7 Whoever possesses faith, morality, harmlessness, abstinence and moderation, of that intelligent and unblemished person it is said: 'He is a model of wisdom.'

Udanavarga 13.12 A man, even if of weak intelligence but who practices morality, is praised by the wise, for his life is pure and unremitting.

Psalm 101.6 Mine eyes shall be upon the faithful of the land, that they may dwell with me: he that walketh in a perfect way, he shall serve me.

Leviticus 19.2 Speak unto all the congregation of the children of Israel, and say unto them, Ye shall be holy: for I the LORD your God am holy.

"Holy" here is KaDoWSH, meaning set apart, distinct, one of a kind, precious. In this next verses, "perfect" is TaMiYM, meaning having integrity, being complete, whole, entire, without any loss, healthy. The "world" is a sick diseased place, spiritually or mentally speaking, but you can be apart from that, you can be well. You can be immune to the bad influences out there.

Genesis 17.1 And when Abram was ninety years old and nine, the LORD appeared to Abram, and said unto him, I am the Almighty God; walk before me, and be thou perfect.

Deuteronomy 18.13 Thou shalt be perfect with the LORD thy God.

1 Kings 8.61 Let your heart therefore be perfect with the LORD our God, to walk in his statutes, and to keep his commandments, as at this day.

1 Chronicles 28.9 And thou, Solomon my son, know thou the God of thy father, and serve him with a perfect heart and with a willing mind: for the LORD searcheth all hearts, and understandeth all the imaginations of the thoughts: if thou seek him, he will be found of thee; but if thou forsake him, he will cast thee off for ever.

Jubilees 5.12 And he made for all his works a new and righteous nature so that they might not sin in all their nature forever, and so that they might all be righteous, each to his kind, always.

Good is natural. Everything other is a collection of accepted lies. So many cherished lies create so much human suffering, political lies, religious lies, media lies, cultural lies, the clinging to antiquated ideas, narrow mindedness, and bigotry. So much to have to unlearn, to let go of, to abandon to get back to the natural innocence from which we should all be operating.

Jeremiah 9.23-24 Thus saith the LORD, Let not the wise man glory in his wisdom, neither let the mighty man glory in his might, let not the rich man glory in his riches: but let him that glorieth glory in this, that he understandeth and knoweth me, that I am the LORD which exercise loving-kindness, judgment, and righteousness, in the earth: for in these things I delight, saith the LORD.

The way I think about these verses is: "This is the word of the Lord (thanks be to God): The wise do not own their own wisdom [CHoKMaH, Sophia], the strong do not own their own strength [GeBuWRaH], the rich do not own their own wealth: because the only thing you can ultimately own is that you have enough prudence and perception to know the God of lovingkindness [CHeSeD] who lives in right words and right rule, across the land with gladness." It was verses like this that inspired Kabbalah, and Gnosticism. To understand and to know are the keys to perfection. To understand car mechanics is key to getting the car to start. To understand the musical instrument is key to playing the song. God is good. Every other concept of God is a lie.

In light of this, to be "perfect as the LORD is perfect" is not about knowing it all, or being almighty strong, or owning it all. It is about compassion and an eye for overcoming injustice, and bringing it all down to earth. This perfection is attainable at any time by anyone. We are all limited in every way except for our immediate and ever present ability to care, to exercise compassion, empathy, charity. This is the only perfection Jesus could be speaking of here.

Lotus Sutra 2 The Buddhas, the World-Honored Ones, wish to open the door of Buddha wisdom to all living beings to allow them to attain purity. [...] The original vow of the Buddhas was that the Buddha way, which they themselves practice, should be shared universally among living beings so that they too may attain this same way.

What if we stopped venerating the Great Teachers of human history enough to instead venerate their message, to venerate actually partaking of their message, venerate walking in their footsteps? To Buddha, the "awakened", we strove to wake up ourselves in mindfulness in our daily lives? To Christ, the "anointed", we strove to anoint ourselves with the same Holy Spirit? To Muhammad, the "prophet", we strove to become channels of the will of God in our own capacities and unique experiences in life? To Lao Tzu, the pointer to "the way", we endeavored to follow "the way" in our own minds? To Krishna, the "avatar", we awakened the god-like qualities within us and drove the chariot of our lives with strength and wisdom? What if for whatever truths we have learned in life, we strove to share them for the benefit of us all?

Bhagavad Gita 18.9 But he who does holy work, Arjuna, because it ought to be done, and surrenders selfishness and thought of reward, his work is pure, and is peace.

Motivation is key. To unplug the concept of working for pay, for reward, for recognition, for position, is to create a pure act that transcends the selfish life and connects to the Compassion that transcends and yet touches us all.

To fulfil the Law can only be accomplished through participating in Love. In this lies perfection. In this seed is planted the Dream.

Prophets' Dreams

This is nothing short of a concise instruction manual on how to be a living prophet for God. You have the blessings like Abraham, the law like Moses, now you need to work on intending your vision, realizing your dream.

Isaiah 11.6 The wolf also shall dwell with the lamb, and the leopard shall lie down with the kid; and the calf and the young lion and the fatling together; and a little child shall lead them.

First off, there is a sense of privacy, anonymity, the exact opposite of those who flaunt their religion. It needs to be a quiet pushing for changes, with no sense of wanting to be praised or acknowledged for the work being done. Everything should be done with acknowledging the hand of God in the work, and God's will being done to bring about heaven on earth in as much as it becomes possible in each situation. The dream should see plenty for all, compassion for all, an end of violence, an end of greed running the world, an end of bigotry, a bringing together the diversity of humanity with a sense of letting go of it all. Enmity fades into forgiveness. Segregation of wealth fades into fasting. It is a complete reversal of values from what the world out there thinks we should want for ourselves and for those around us. In this dream, we redefine what we treasure, redefine vision. We redefine identifications of what we choose to allow to master us in life. We stop worrying so much, stop being so judgmental, and all agree to deal fairly and honestly in all situations.

We are instructed to protect our cherished sacred vision from the profane, to actively seek out the sacred and apply it to all as we see fit. We are instructed to be wise and distinguish paths and their destinations, to thus be wary of religious and political movements that promote hatred and divisions. What we build and leave behind as our legacies should be based on these founding principles, rooted in direct experience and not just in blind faith, real heart-felt spiritual maturity and not just going through the motions and appearances of being religious.

See the Need

Shepherd of Hermas Parable 10 4.2-4 Charge all men who are able to do right, that they cease not to practice good works; for it is useful for them. I say moreover that every man ought to be rescued from misfortune; for he that hath need, and suffereth misfortune in his daily life, is in great torment and want. Whosoever therefore rescueth from penury a life of this kind, winneth great joy for himself. For he who is harassed by misfortune of this sort is afflicted and tortured with equal torment as one who is in chains. For many men on account of calamities of this kind, because they can bear them no longer, lay violent hands on themselves. He then who knows the calamity of a man of this kind and rescueth him not, committeth great sin, and becometh guilty of the man's blood. Do therefore good works, whoever of you have received benefits from the Lord, lest, while ye delay to do them, the building of the tower be completed. For it is on your account that the work of the building has been interrupted. Unless then ye hasten to do right, the tower will be completed, and ye shut out."

Avoid Religious Hypocrisy

Matthew 6.1 Take heed that ye do not your alms before men, to be seen of them: otherwise ye have no reward of your Father which is in heaven.

In some versions "alms" is changed to "acts of righteousness". In Aramaic the word "ZaDoK" can be translated either way. This may indicate that there was an Aramaic original to this text.

Matthew 6.2 Therefore when thou doest thine alms, do not sound a trumpet before thee, as the hypocrites do in the synagogues and in the streets, that they may have glory of men. Verily I say unto you, They have their reward.

Matthew 6.3 But when thou doest alms, let not thy left hand know what thy right hand doeth:

Matthew 6.4 That thine alms may be in secret: and thy Father which seeth in secret himself shall reward thee openly.

Matthew 6.5 And when thou prayest, thou shalt not be as the hypocrites are: for they love to pray standing in the synagogues and in the corners of the streets, that they may be seen of men. Verily I say unto you, They have their reward.

Tao Te Ching 7 The sage stays behind, thus he is ahead. He is detached, thus at one with all. Through selfless action, he attains fulfillment.

Apollonius of Tyana: Letter 32: To the scribes of the Ephesians: Multicolored stones and paintings, walkways, and theaters are useless in a city unless it also contains wisdom and law. Such things are the subject of wisdom and law, not equivalent to them.

Apollonius of Tyana 1.11.2 [Hypocrites] do not make these sacrifices and dedications to honor divinity, but to buy a favorable judgment, which you gods in your great justice do not grant.

AL BAQARAH 2.264 O ye who believe! Cancel not your charity by reminders of your generosity or by injury – like those who spend their substance to be seen of men, but believe neither in Allah nor in the Last Day. They are in parable like a hard, barren rock, on which is a little soil: on it falls heavy rain, which leaves it (just) a bare stone. They will be able to do nothing with aught they have earned. And Allah guideth not those who reject faith.

AL BAQARAH 2.271 If ye disclose (acts of) charity, even so it is well, but if ye conceal them, and make them reach those (really) in need, that is best for you: It will remove from you some of your (stains of) evil. And Allah is well acquainted with what ye do.

AL 'ANKABUT 29.11 And Allah most certainly knows those who believe, and as certainly those who are Hypocrites.

AL NISA' 4.142 The Hypocrites – they think they are over-reaching Allah, but He will over-reach them: When they stand up to prayer, they stand without earnestness, to be seen of men, but little do they hold Allah in remembrance;

AL MA'UN 107.4-7 So woe to the worshippers who are neglectful of their prayers, those who (want but) to be seen (of men), but refuse (to supply) (even) neighbourly needs.

Samanamandika Sutta 11 Here a bhikkhu is virtuous, but he does not identify with his virtue, and he understands as it actually is that deliverance of mind and deliverance by wisdom where these wholesome habits cease without remainder.

Bhagavad Gita 2.42-44 There are men who have no vision, and yet they speak many words. They follow the letter of the Vedas, and they say. 'there is nothing but this.' Their soul is warped with selfish desires and their heaven is a selfish desire. They have prayers for pleasures and power, the reward of which is earthly rebirth. Those who love pleasure and power hear and follow their words: they have not the determination ever to be one with the One.

Bhagavad Gita 5.12 The man of harmony surrenders the reward of his work and thus attains final peace: the man of disharmony, urged by desire, is attached to his reward and remains in bondage.

Bhagavad Gita 18.5-6 Works of sacrifice, gift, and self-harmony should not be abandoned, but should indeed be performed; for these are works of purification. But even these works, Arjuna, should be done in the freedom of a pure offering, and without expectation of a reward. This is my final word.

For show or for real? Faith or gnosis? Follow men or experience it for yourself? Collect many words, study about it, contemplate it, or hands on experience of being One with it? On the screen or sitting in your lap? Nothing but the Vedas. Nothing but the Bible. The hypocrisy of religious institution. Getting it real is something much different from established religion. Actually doing some good. Actually connecting to something real and not just imagined or hoped for. Real alms. Real prayer. God realization. To do good not for credit or for any recognition, but to do it because it is the right thing to do, surrendered, harmonious, is freeing in a way that no other action could accomplish. Perfect alms. Not even the left hand knows what good the right hand is doing. Really helping someone in need is spiritual self-therapy.

Bhagavad Gita 18.11-12 For there is no man on earth who can fully renounce living work, but he who renounces the reward of his work is in truth a man of renunciation. When work is done for a reward, the work brings pleasure, or pain, or both, in its time; but when a man does work in Eternity, then Eternity is his reward.

In Private

Matthew 6.6 But thou, when thou prayest, enter into thy closet, and when thou hast shut thy door, pray to thy Father which is in secret; and thy Father which seeth in secret shall reward thee openly.

Bhagavad Gita 6.10 Day after day, let the Yogi practise the harmony of soul. in a secret place, in deep solitude, master of his mind, hoping for nothing, desiring nothing.

Tao Te Ching 47 Without going outside, you may know the whole world. Without looking through the window, you may see the ways of heaven.

This thought from the Tao Te Ching inspired The Inner Light song by George Harrison of the Beatles.

Isaiah 26.20 Come, my people, enter thou into thy chambers, and shut thy doors about thee: hide thyself as it were for a little moment, until the indignation be overpast.

John 6.15 When Jesus therefore perceived that they would come and take him by force, to make him a king, he departed again into a mountain himself alone.

Matthew 14.23 Sending the crowds away he went up into the hills by himself to pray.

Mark 1.35 And in the morning, rising up a great while before day, he went out, and departed into a solitary place, and there prayed.

Luke 5.16 And he [Jesus] withdrew himself into the wilderness and prayed.

Luke 9.18 And it came to pass, as he [Jesus] was alone praying, his disciples were with him: and he asked them, saying, Whom say the people that I am?

Matthew 26.36 Remain here while I go off alone to pray.

Mahapadana Sutta 2.17 It is not proper for me to live with a crowd like this. I must live alone, withdrawn from this crowd.

Culasaropama Sutta 13 Here, Brahmin, quite secluded from sensual pleasures, secluded from unwholesome states, a bhikkhu enters upon and abides in the first jhana [meditative state], which is accompanied by applied and sustained thought, with rapture and pleasure born of seclusion. This is a state higher and more sublime than knowledge and vision.

There are too many bad influences out there. If you can't find friends who are not bad influences, you are better off going solo in life.

Without a Lot of Words

Matthew 6.7 But when ye pray, use not vain repetitions, as the heathen do: for they think that they shall be heard for their much speaking.

Matthew 6.8 Be not ye therefore like unto them: for your Father knoweth what things ye have need of, before ye ask him.

Some versions have "God your Father".

Kandaraka Sutta 18, Maha-Assapura Sutta 12 Possessing this aggregate of noble virtue, and this noble restraint of the faculties, and possessing this noble mindfulness and full awareness, he resorts to a secluded resting place: the forest, the root of a tree, a mountain, a ravine, a hillside cave, a charnel ground, a jungle thicket, an open space, a heap of straw.

Mahasunnata Sutta 3 Ananda, a bhikkhu does not shine by delighting in company, by taking delight in company, by devoting himself to delight in company; by delighting in society, by taking delight in society, by rejoicing in society.

Khandhasamyutta 81 After his meal he set his lodging in order himself, took his bowl and robe, and without informing his personal attendants, without taking leave of the Bhikkhu Sangha, he set out on tour alone, without a companion.

Culasunnata Sutta 4 A bhikkhu – not attending to the perception of village, not attending to the perception of people – attends to the singleness dependent on the perception of forest. His mind enters into that perception of forest. His mind enters into that perception of forest and acquires confidence, steadiness, and decision.

Upakkilesa Sutta If one can find a worthy friend, a virtuous, steadfast companion, then overcome all threats of danger and walk with him content and mindful. But if one finds no worthy friend, no virtuous, steadfast companion, then as a king leaves his conquered realm, walk like a tusker in the woods alone. Better it is to walk alone, there is no companionship with fools. Walk alone and do no evil, at ease like a tusker in the woods.

Thomas 49 Jesus said, "Blessed are the solitary and elect, for you will find the kingdom. For you are from it, and to it you will return."

Marasamyutta 25 Defeated is the army of pleasant and agreeable contacts. Meditating alone, I discover a blissful attainment of my goal, a heart at rest. Thus I avoid closeness with people, not forming intimate ties.

Dhammadayada Sutta 6 Here disciples of the Teacher who lives secluded do not train in seclusion; they do not abandon what the Teacher tells them to abandon; they are luxurious and careless, leaders in backsliding, neglectful of seclusion.

Thoughts come to mind here: vision quest, retreat, monastic life. Gathered loud zealots are the seed for violent revolution, terrorist activity, and religious crusades. Such public display of religious fervor occupied Jerusalem with God on their side, and lost. Isolated quiet contemplators of higher truths remained in the aftermath of death and destruction, better people and much less volatile. We don't need another violent revolution. We need revolutions of common sense, of compassion, of embracing differences, of actual and effective charity. See what all that praying for victory got them.

Prayer

Matthew 6.9 After this manner therefore pray ye: Our Father which art in heaven, Hallowed be thy name.

Tobit 13.4 There declare his greatness, and extol him before all the living: for he is our Lord, and he is the God our Father for ever.

Didache 8.2-3 And do not pray as the hypocrites, but as the Lord commanded in his Gospel, pray thus: "Our Father, who art in Heaven, hallowed be thy Name, thy Kingdom come, thy will be done, as in Heaven so also upon earth; give us to-day our daily bread, and forgive us our debt as we forgive our debtors, and lead us not into trial, but deliver us from the Evil One, for thine is the power and the glory for ever." Pray thus three times a day.

Corpus Hermeticum 14.7 Nothing evil or shameful can be ascribed to the Creator. These are afflictions which follow upon coming into being, like the green on copper and dirt on the body. For the coppersmith does not make the green, not the parents the dirt on the body, nor does God create evil.

AL NAML 27.3 Those who establish regular prayers and give in regular charity, and also have (full) assurance of the hereafter.

AL NUR 24.56 So establish regular Prayer and give regular Charity; and obey the Messenger; that ye may receive mercy.

AL MU'MINUN 23.1-2 The believers must (eventually) win through – those who humble themselves in their prayers.

AL MU'MINUN 23.8-11 Those who faithfully observe their trusts and their covenants; and who (strictly) guard their prayers;-these will be the heirs, who will inherit Paradise: they will dwell therein (for ever).

The prayer isn't begging God to give you something or fix something for you. The prayer is to respect the sacred. The Great Cosmic Word (name) is our generator, our founder, our source for the sacred.

Kingdom Come

Matthew 6.10 Thy kingdom come. Thy will be done in earth, as it is in heaven.

Basileia – dominion, rule, influence, this is the Greek word translated as kingdom. This great cosmic force can be connected to, grounded through us. Thelema is the Greek for "will", determination, wishes, desire. 93 is the numerical value in Greek both for thelema and for agape – the will of God and the love of God.

Ezekiel 36.22-26 Therefore say unto the house of Israel, Thus saith the Lord GOD; I do not this for your sakes, O house of Israel, but for mine holy name's sake, which ye have profaned among the heathen, whither ye went. And I will sanctify my great name, which was profaned among the heathen, which ye have profaned in the midst of them; and the heathen shall know that I am the LORD, saith the Lord GOD, when I shall be sanctified in you before their eyes. For I will take you from among the heathen, and gather you out of all countries, and will bring you into your own land. Then will I sprinkle clean water upon you, and ye shall be clean: from all your filthiness, and from all your idols, will I cleanse you. A new heart also will I give you, and a new spirit will I put within you: and I will take away the stony heart out of your flesh, and I will give you an heart of flesh.

The Jewish tradition had been profaned by violence, by xenophobia. The tradition had to be washed, baptized, reformed, and refocused. The influence (kingdom, basileia in Greek) is to be evident in the world by appreciation of values, not by force of violent means.

Daniel 4.3 How great are his signs! And how mighty are his wonders! His kingdom is an everlasting kingdom, and his dominion is from generation to generation.

Abu 'Abdallah Ahmad b. Muhammad al-Shaybani Ibn Hanbal: Kitab al-Zuhd 484 Christ said, "Not as I will but as You will. Not as I desire but as You desire."

Daily Bread

Matthew 6.11 Give us this day our daily bread.

Matthew 6.12 And forgive us our debts, as we forgive our debtors.

Food for physical hunger, forgiveness for spiritual shortcomings, energy for life, energy for mind, we feed from the ultimate Parent. We run with a healthy body and intend though a confident spirit, for we have been fed. This will of God, this love of God feeds us, purifies us, transforms us.

Abu 'Abdallah Ahmad b. Muhammad al-Shaybani Ibn Hanbal: Kitab al-Zuhd 302 Christ said, "Make frequent mention of God the Exalted, also of His praise and glorification, and obey Him. It suffices for one of you when praying, and if God is truly pleased with him, to say: 'O God, forgive my sins, reform my way of life, and keep me safe from hateful things, O my God.'"

AL SHU'ARA 26.77-82 For they are enemies to me; not so the Lord and Cherisher of the Worlds; who created me, and it is He who guides me; who gives me food and drink, and when I am ill, it is He who cures me; who will cause me to die, and then to life (again); and who, I hope, will forgive me my faults on the day of Judgment.

Ezekiel 36.27-30 And I will put my spirit within you, and cause you to walk in my statutes, and ye shall keep my judgments, and do them. And ye shall dwell in the land that I gave to your fathers; and ye shall be my people, and I will be your God. I will also save you from all your uncleannesses: and I will call for the corn, and will increase it, and lay no famine upon you. And I will multiply the fruit of the tree, and the increase of the field, that ye shall receive no more reproach of famine among the heathen.

Proverbs 30.7-9 Two things have I required of thee; deny me them not before I die: Remove far from me vanity and lies: give me neither poverty nor riches; feed me with food convenient for me: Lest I be full, and deny thee, and say, Who is the LORD? Or lest I be poor, and steal, and take the name of my God in vain.

Deliver us from Evil

Matthew 6.13 And lead us not into temptation, but deliver us from evil: For thine is the kingdom, and the power, and the glory, for ever. Amen.

AL NAS 114.1-4 Say: I seek refuge with the Lord and cherisher of mankind, the King (or Ruler) of mankind, the God (or Judge) of mankind, from the mischief of the Whisperer (of Evil), who withdraws (after his whisper).

Evil in Greek here is poneros, which is much like what Buddha called suffering, dukkha in Pali, with the connotations of bad conditioning, disease, annoyance, peril. God is our deliverer, our rescuer, our distractor from the path of temptation that has brought us so much suffering. Deliverance from suffering is not so much the protection of a strong force from this external peril as it is a strengthening of will power to overcome the temptations that distract us from how we are destined to be. Being within the extant of the influence, the kingdom come, is to feel the power and the brilliance of being in this zone. Gone are the temptations and distractions, thus gone is the suffering. Then, from within whatever situation we find ourselves to be in, we can stand strong in the storm and shine in the darkness because we are connected.

AL INSAN 76.11 But Allah will deliver them from the evil of that Day, and will shed over them a Light of Beauty and (blissful) Joy.

What exactly were the evils to be delivered from was well defined in early Christianity. In modern movies, the concept of evil takes on the form of some monster out there to be dealt with. The real demons to run past are found within, and we let them haunt us and control us, tempt us and lead us into situations that we would rather avoid. What we need is the strength, the antidote, the healing process to begin within us.

Didache 5.1-2 But the Way of Death is this: First of all, it is wicked and full of cursing, murders, adulteries, lusts, fornications, thefts, idolatries, witchcrafts, charms, robberies, false witness, hypocrisies, a double heart, fraud, pride, malice, stubbornness, covetousness, foul speech, jealousy, impudence, haughtiness, boastfulness. Persecutors of the good, haters of truth, lovers of lies, knowing not the reward of righteousness, not cleaving to the good nor to righteous judgment, spending wakeful nights not for good but for wickedness, from whom meekness and patience is far, lovers of vanity, following after reward, unmerciful to the poor, not working for him who is oppressed with toil, without knowledge of him who made them, murderers of children, corrupters of God's creatures, turning away the needy, oppressing the distressed, advocates of the rich, unjust judges of the poor, altogether sinful; may ye be delivered, my children, from all these.

Barnabas 20.1-2 But the way of the Black One is crooked and full of a curse. For it is a way of eternal death with punishment wherein are the things that destroy men's souls – idolatry, boldness, exhalation of power, hypocrisy, doubleness of heart, adultery, murder, plundering, pride, transgression, treachery, malice, stubbornness, witchcraft, magic, covetousness, absence of the fear of God; persecutors of good men, hating the truth, loving lies, not perceiving the reward of righteousness, not cleaving to the good nor to the righteous judgment, paying no heed to the widow and the orphan, wakeful not for the fear of God but for that which is evil; men from whom gentleness and forbearance stand aloof and far off; loving vain things, pursuing a recompense, not pitying the poor man, not toiling for him that is oppressed with toil, ready to slander, not recognizing Him that made them, murderers of children, corrupters of the creatures of God, turning away from him that is in want, oppressing him that is afflicted, advocates of the wealthy, unjust judges of the poor, sinful in all things.

Psalm 140.1 <To the chief Musician, A Psalm of David.> Deliver me, O LORD, from the evil man: preserve me from the violent man;

Proverbs 2.12 To deliver thee from the way of the evil man, from the man that speaketh froward things;

Dead Sea Scrolls 4Q525 Frag 14 2.11-12 You shall love God with all your heart and with all your soul. He shall deliver you from every evil, and terror shall not bring you down.

Jeremiah 21.12 O house of David, thus saith the LORD; Execute judgment in the morning, and deliver him that is spoiled out of the hand of the oppressor, lest my fury go out like fire, and burn that none can quench it, because of the evil of your doings.

There is this Sunday School idea that the Jews were good and the Romans were evil: the good Jews needed to be delivered from the oppressive occupation of the heathen Romans. What Josephus illustrates in his writings is that from another perspective, the evil that needed to be delivered from was that of the violent revolutionary Zealots. In what seems to modern thought to be a twisted way of looking at it, when Titus arrived in Jerusalem to defeat the Zealots, he was actually doing God a favor, delivering the Roman world from the evil terrorists.

Forgiven

Matthew 6.14 For if ye forgive men their trespasses, your heavenly Father will also forgive you:

AL NISA' 4.110 If any one does evil or wrongs his own soul but afterwards seeks Allah's forgiveness, he will find Allah Oft-forgiving, Most Merciful.

Ezekiel 36.31-33 Then shall ye remember your own evil ways, and your doings that were not good, and shall lothe yourselves in your own sight for your iniquities and for your abominations. Not for your sakes do I this, saith the Lord GOD, be it known unto you: be ashamed and confounded for your own ways, O house of Israel. Thus saith the Lord GOD; In the day that I shall have cleansed you from all your iniquities I will also cause you to dwell in the cities, and the wastes shall be builded.

Abu 'Uthman 'Amr b. Bahr Al-Jahiz: Al-Bayan wa al-Tabyin 1.399 Christ came upon a group of people who were crying. He asked, "Why are these people crying?" He was told, "They are afraid of their sins." He said, "Abandon them and you will be forgiven."

Gamanisamyutta 8 When the liberation of mind by lovingkindness is developed and cultivated in this way, any limited karma that was done does not remain there, does not persist there.

TA HA 20.82 "But, without doubt, I am (also) He that forgives again and again, to those who repent, believe, and do right – who, in fine, are ready to receive true guidance."

AL SHURA 42.25 He is the One that accepts repentance from His Servants and forgives sins: and He knows all that ye do.

AL NAML 27.11 "But if any have done wrong and have thereafter substituted good to take the place of evil, truly, I am Oft-Forgiving, Most Merciful.

AL QASAS 28.16 He prayed: "O my Lord! I have indeed wronged my soul! Do Thou then forgive me!" So (Allah) forgave him: for He is the Oft-Forgiving, Most Merciful.

AL HAJJ 22.50 "Those who believe and work righteousness, for them is forgiveness and a sustenance most generous.

AL 'IMRAN 3.31 Say: "If ye do love Allah, Follow me: Allah will love you and forgive you your sins: For Allah is Oft-Forgiving, Most Merciful."

God is forgiving. God is rebuilding. God is restoring. The offness we feel comes from ourselves, our collections of substitutes and lies. Once we unlearn the lies and get back to the innocence, God stands forever forgiving and nurturing. This is perhaps the greatest insight Muhammad ever had.

Forgive

Matthew 6.15 But if ye forgive not men their trespasses, neither will your Father forgive your trespasses.

Obstacle one in religion: being judgmental.

John 8.7 So when they continued asking him, he lifted up himself, and said unto them, He that is without sin among you, let him first cast a stone at her.

Sirach 28.1-4 He that revengeth shall find vengeance from the Lord, and he will surely keep his sins in remembrance. Forgive thy neighbour the hurt that he hath done unto thee, so shall thy sins also be forgiven when thou prayest. One man beareth hatred against another, and doth he seek pardon from the Lord? He sheweth no mercy to a man, which is like himself: and doth he ask forgiveness of his own sins?

Devatasamyutta 35 If one does not grant pardon to those who confess transgression, angry at heart, intent on hate, one strongly harbours enmity. In that enmity I do not delight, thus I pardon your transgression.

Sakkasamyutta 24 There are two types of fools: one who does not see a transgression as a transgression; and one who, when another is confessing a transgression, does not pardon him.

Fasting

Matthew 6.16 Moreover when ye fast, be not, as the hypocrites, of a sad countenance: for they disfigure their faces, that they may appear unto men to fast. Verily I say unto you, They have their reward.

Matthew 6.17 But thou, when thou fastest, anoint thine head, and wash thy face;

Matthew 6.18 That thou appear not unto men to fast, but unto thy Father which is in secret: and thy Father, which seeth in secret, shall reward thee openly.

Obstacle two in religion: having it become for show.

Hypocrites is a word derived from the Greek hupokrites, which basically means an actor in a play. What Jesus here is critiquing are those who act the part of religion, and yet show no understanding of the heart behind the rituals and words. Learning to recite the words and partake in the rituals is meaningless without the accompanying gnosis of the meaning.

Isaiah 58.5-12 Is it such a fast that I have chosen? A day for a man to afflict his soul? Is it to bow down his head as a bulrush, and to spread sackcloth and ashes under him? Wilt thou call this a fast, and an acceptable day to the LORD? Is not this the fast that I have chosen? To loose the bands of wickedness, to undo the heavy burdens, and to let the oppressed go free, and that ye break every yoke? Is it not to deal thy bread to the hungry, and that thou bring the poor that are cast out to thy house? When thou seest the naked, that thou cover him; and that thou hide not thyself from thine own flesh? Then shall thy light break forth as the morning, and thine health shall spring forth speedily: and thy righteousness shall go before thee; the glory of the LORD shall be thy reward. Then shalt thou call, and the LORD shall answer; thou shalt cry, and he shall say, Here I am. If thou take away from the midst of thee the yoke, the putting forth of the finger, and speaking vanity; And if thou draw out thy soul to the hungry, and satisfy the afflicted soul; then shall thy light rise in obscurity, and thy darkness be as the noonday: And the LORD shall guide thee continually, and satisfy thy soul in drought, and make fat thy bones: and thou shalt be like a watered garden, and like a spring of water, whose waters fail not. And they that shall be of thee shall build the old waste places: thou shalt raise up the foundations of many generations; and thou shalt be called, The repairer of the breach, The restorer of paths to dwell in.

Treasures upon Earth

Matthew 6.19 Lay not up for yourselves treasures upon earth, where moth and rust doth corrupt, and where thieves break through and steal:

Obstacle three in religion: religious show of wealth. The grand expensive churches do not represent the heart of Jesus here.

Lotus Sutra 18 I must now teach them so they can gain the fruits of the way! Immediately for their sake he employs an expedient means, preaching the true Law of nirvana: Nothing in this world is lasting or firm but are like bubbles, foam, heat shimmer. Therefore all of you must quickly learn to hate it and be gone!

Ratthapala Sutta 42 And as he dies, no relatives or friends can offer him shelter and refuge here. While his heirs take over his wealth, this being must pass on according to his actions; and as he dies nothing can follow him; not child nor wife nor wealth nor royal estate.

Mahadukkhakklandha Sutta 10 If property comes to the clansman whiles he works and strives and makes an effort thus, he experiences pain and grief in protecting it: 'How shall neither kings nor thieves make off with my property, nor fire burn it, nor water sweep it away, nor hateful heirs make off with it?' And as he guards and protects his property, kings or thieves make off with it, or fire burns it, or water sweeps it away, or hateful heirs make off with it. And he sorrows, grieves, and laments, he weeps beating his breast and becomes distraught, crying: 'What I had I have no longer!'

Tevijjavacchagotta Sutta 11 Vacca, there is no householder who, without abandoning the fetter of householdership, on the dissolution of the body has made an end of suffering.

Vangisasamyutta 2 Whatever exists here on earth and in space, comprised by form, included in the world – everything impermanent decays; the sages fare having pierced this truth. People are tied to their acquisitions, to what is seen, heard, sensed, and felt; dispel desire for this, be unstirred: they call him a sage who clings to nothing here.

Ratthapala Sutta 22 Householder, if you follow my advice, then have this pile of gold coins and bullion loaded on carts and carried away to be dumped midstream in the river Ganges. Why is that? Because, householder, on account of this there will arise for you sorrow, lamentation, pain, grief, and despair.

Devatasamyutta 41 When one's house is ablaze the vessel taken out is the one that is useful, not the one left burnt inside. So when the world is ablaze with the fires of aging and death, one should take out one's wealth by giving: what is given is well salvaged. What is given yields pleasant fruit, but not so what is not given. Thieves take it away, or kings, it gets burnt by fire or is lost.

Dhammapada 13.11 Misers certainly do not go to the heaven of the gods, and fools do not praise liberality; but noble men find joy in generosity, and this gives them joy in higher worlds.

Udanavarga 1.22 All accumulations end in ruin; all elevations in fall; unions end in separation, life ends in death.

Dialogue of the Saviour 44 Strive to save that which can follow you, and to seek it out, and to speak from within it, so that, as you seek it out, everything might be in harmony with you.

James 5.1-3 Go to now, ye rich men, weep and howl for your miseries that shall come upon you. Your riches are corrupted, and your garments are motheaten. Your gold and silver is cankered; and the rust of them shall be a witness against you, and shall eat your flesh as it were fire. Ye have heaped treasure together for the last days.

Corpus Hermeticum 13.7 Withdraw into yourself and it shall come. Will and it is so. Make idle the senses of the body and the spirit will be born. Cleanse yourself from the torments of the material world which arise from the lack of reason.

Psalm 37.4 Delight thyself also in the LORD; and he shall give thee the desires of thine heart.

AL HUMAZAH 104.2-3 Who pileth up wealth and layeth it by, thinking that his wealth would make him last for ever!

Abu 'Abdallah Ahmad b. Muhammad al-Shaybani Ibn Hanbal: Kitab al-Zuhd 474 Jesus said, "In truth I say to you, the folds of heaven are empty of the rich. It is easier for a camel to pass through the eye of a needle than for a rich man to enter paradise."

Svetasvatara Upanishad 1 Matter in time passes away, but God is for ever in Eternity, and he rules both matter and soul. By meditation on him, by contemplation of him, and by communion with him, there comes in the end the destruction of earthly delusion.

Abu 'Abdallah Ahmad b. Muhammad al-Shaybani Ibn Hanbal: Kitab al-Zuhd 402 Jesus said, "What God loves most are the strangers." He was asked, "Who are the strangers?" He replied, "Those who flee the world with their faith intact." They shall be gathered together with Jesus on the Day of Judgment.

AL SHURA 42.20 To any that desires the tilth of the Hereafter, We give increase in his tilth, and to any that desires the tilth of this world, We grant somewhat thereof, but he has no share or lot in the Hereafter.

Tilth is dirt that is ready to produce an abundance of crops, a fertile place to grow what you want to be grown. If you want a field of barley, you need to find a good acre of dirt and plant your barley seed. If you want to grow spiritual barley, you need to arrange to get enough spiritual dirt that is ready and fertile enough to grow your crop. Whatever you grow is going to take a lot of your time and energy.

Alagaddupama Sutta 3 The Blessed One has stated how sensual pleasures provide little gratification, much suffering, and much despair, and how great is the danger in them.

Bhagavad Gita 18.37-38 What seems at first a cup of sorrow is found in the end immortal wine. That pleasure is pure: it is the joy which arises from a clear vision of the Spirit. But the pleasure which comes from the craving of the senses with the objects of their desire, which seems at first a drink of sweetness but is found in the end a cup of poison, is the pleasure of passion, impure.

Defining what you treasure, the slowing down of the spinning of living for pleasures, realigning values, is a theme in every form of mysticism throughout the world and in every age and culture. As long as everyone wants so much stuff and fights to afford it and fights to protect it, there will never be peace. To control may lead to violence. To crave may lead to theft, manipulation, deprivation of someone else's cravings. The Wheel is in motion and there is no way to stop it when you are contributing to keeping it in motion by playing its game.

Isaiah 51.7-11 Hearken unto me, ye that know righteousness, the people in whose heart is my law; fear ye not the reproach of men, neither be ye afraid of their revilings. For the moth shall eat them up like a garment, and the worm shall eat them like wool: but my righteousness shall be for ever, and my salvation from generation to generation. Awake, awake, put on strength, O arm of the LORD; awake, as in the ancient days, in the generations of old. Art thou not it that hath cut Rahab, and wounded the dragon? Art thou not it which hath dried the sea, the waters of the great deep; that hath made the depths of the sea a way for the ransomed to pass over? Therefore the redeemed of the LORD shall return, and come with singing unto Zion; and everlasting joy shall be upon their head: they shall obtain gladness and joy; and sorrow and mourning shall flee away.

For a man seeking a beautiful woman, when a beautiful woman appears before him, he doesn't care about any other distractions. When a person is hungry, food takes on focus. When a person needs money, getting paid takes on priority. Spiritual gnosis is like this. You have to value it to where it is more important to you than anything else. You don't treasure what they treasure any more as much as you value your new obsession. And you don't flaunt your new passion with showiness of their definition of wealth and success and influence. Never forget, you are not playing their game. It doesn't matter if they win, because you are not playing.

Looking Two Directions

Abu 'Uthman 'Amr b. Bahr Al-Jahiz: Al-Bayan wa al-Tabyin 3.166 Jesus said, "You work for this world, where you are provided for without working; whereas you do not work for the afterlife, where you will not be provided for except by working."

Katha Upanishad 4 The Creator made the senses outward going: they go to the world of matter outside, not to the Spirit within. But a sage who sought immortality looked within himself and found his own Soul. The foolish run after outward pleasures and fall into the snares of vast-embracing death. But the wise have found immortality, and do not seek the Eternal in things that pass away.

GHAFIR 40.39 "O my people! This life of the present is nothing but (temporary) convenience: It is the Hereafter that is the Home that will last.

AL QASAS 28.60 The (material) things which ye are given are but the conveniences of this life and the glitter thereof; but that which is with Allah is better and more enduring: will ye not then be wise?

AL TAWBAH 9.38 O ye who believe! what is the matter with you, that, when ye are asked to go forth in the cause of Allah, ye cling heavily to the earth? Do ye prefer the life of this world to the Hereafter? But little is the comfort of this life, as compared with the Hereafter.

AL 'IMRAN 3.14 Fair in the eyes of men is the love of things they covet: Women and sons; Heaped-up hoards of gold and silver; horses branded (for blood and excellence); and (wealth of) cattle and well-tilled land. Such are the possessions of this world's life; but in nearness to Allah is the best of the goals (to return to).

YUNUS 10.58 Say: "In the bounty of Allah. And in His Mercy – in that let them rejoice": that is better than the (wealth) they hoard.

AL SHURA 42.36 Whatever ye are given (here) is (but) a convenience of this life: but that which is with Allah is better and more lasting: (it is) for those who believe and put their trust in their Lord:

Matthew 19.21 Jesus said unto him, If thou wilt be perfect, go and sell that thou hast, and give to the poor, and thou shalt have treasure in heaven: and come and follow me.

Dialogue of the Saviour 55 You are from the fullness and you dwell in the place where the deficiency is. And lo! His light has poured down upon me!

Dialogue of the Saviour 57 When what is alive leaves what is dead, what is alive will be called upon.

Ratthapala Sutta 42 Longevity is not acquired with wealth nor can prosperity banish old age; short is this life, as all the sages say, eternity it knows not, only change. The rich and poor alike shall feel Death's touch, the fool and sage lies stricken by his folly, no sage will ever tremble at the touch. Better is wisdom here than any wealth, since by wisdom one gains the final goal.

Treasures in Heaven

Matthew 6.20 But lay up for yourselves treasures in heaven, where neither moth nor rust doth corrupt, and where thieves do not break through nor steal:

Devatasamyutta 51 Wisdom is the precious gem of humans; merit is hard for thieves to steal.

Proverbs 24.7 Wisdom is too high for a fool: he openeth not his mouth in the gate.

The way I think about this verse is: "For a fool, Sophia is a locked gate that is not asked to be opened."

Proverbs 14.33 Wisdom resteth in the heart of him that hath understanding: but that which is in the midst of fools is made known.

Thomas 76 Jesus said, "The kingdom of the father is like a merchant who had a consignment of merchandise and who discovered a pearl. That merchant was shrewd. He sold the merchandise and bought the pearl alone for himself. You too, seek his unfailing and enduring treasure where no moth comes near to devour and no worm destroys."

Wisdom of Solomon 7.14 For she is a treasure unto men that never faileth: which they that use become the friends of God, being commended for the gifts that come from learning.

Apollonius of Tyana 6.11.12 When philosophy is constituted in the way Pythagoras ordained, and is divinely inspired in the way the Indians ordained before Pythagoras, then the gratitude lasts not for a short time, but for a time beyond number and infinite.

Isaiah 33.6 And wisdom and knowledge shall be the stability of thy times, and strength of salvation: the fear of the LORD is his treasure.

Tobit 12.8-10 Prayer is good with fasting and alms and righteousness. A little with righteousness is better than much with unrighteousness. It is better to give alms than to lay up gold: For alms doth deliver from death, and shall purge away all sin. Those that exercise alms and righteousness shall be filled with life: But they that sin are enemies to their own life.

Proverbs 16.16 How much better is it to get wisdom than gold! And to get understanding rather than silver!

The way I think about this verse is: "CHoKMaH is worth more than gold. BiYNaH is worth more than silver." As Kabbalah terms, these are on top of the chart.

Proverbs 4.5 Get wisdom, get understanding: forget it not; neither decline from the words of my mouth.

The way I think about this verse is: "CHoKMaH and BiYNaH should be guarded in the mind, their advice never ignored or forgotten."

Proverbs 4.7-8 Wisdom is the principal thing: therefore get wisdom: and with all thy getting get understanding. Exalt her, and she shall promote thee: she shall bring thee to honour, when thou doest embrace her.

The way I think about this verse is: "CHoKMaH comes first, and with it BiYNaH naturally comes. Hold her close and she will make you great. Embrace her and she will make you proud." This is a Kabbalistic distinction of these Hebrew words. CHoKMaH is like a skillset earned by persevering in a task, wisdom gained from the experience, from the gnosis. BiYNaH is more of an intuitive knowing, an instinctual understanding, a gift of insight. Not to get too deep in Kabbalah philosophy here, but the Sermon on the Mount is understood in terms of the synergy between these two divine attributes. These are the ultimate treasures.

Udanavarga 10.10-11 Whoever has the wish to see the Noble Ones, who delights in hearing the Good Doctrine, and who has dispelled the stains of avarice, is called a man of faith. As provisions the man of faith carries merit, which it is very difficult for thieves to steal.

Bhagavad Gita 3.16-17 Thus was the Wheel of the Law set in motion, and that man lives indeed in vain who in a sinful life of pleasures helps not in [stopping] its revolutions. But the man who has found the joy of the Spirit and in the Spirit has satisfaction, who in the Spirit has found his peace, that man is beyond the law of action.

Bhagavad Gita 5.3 Know that a man of true renunciation is he who craves not nor hates; for he who is above the two contraries soon finds his freedom.

Abu 'Abdallah Ahmad b. Muhammad al-Shaybani Ibn Hanbal: Kitab al-Zuhd 468 God revealed to Jesus: "Make me your sole concern. Make me as your treasure for your afterlife. Trust in me and I shall suffice you. Do not take anyone else to be your lord, or I shall abandon you."

Hidden Treasure (Buddhist Parables)

Tathagata-garbha Sutra It is like pure honey in a cave or a tree, surrounded and protected by a countless swarm of bees. It may happen that a person comes along who knows some clever techniques. He first gets rid of the bees and takes the honey, and then does as he will with it, eating it or giving it away far and wide.

Tathagata-garbha Sutra It is like a kernel of wheat that has not yet had its husk removed. Someone who is impoverished might foolishly disdain it, and consider it to be something that should be discarded. But when it is cleaned, the kernel can always be used.

Tathagata-garbha Sutra It is like the genuine gold that has fallen into a pit of waste and been submerged and not seen for years. The pure gold does not decay, yet no one knows that it is there. But suppose there came along someone with supernatural vision, who told people, 'Within the impure waste there is a genuine gold trinket. You should get it out and do with it as you please.'

Tathagata-garbha Sutra It is like a store of treasure hidden beneath an impoverished household. The treasure cannot speak and say that it is there, since it isn't conscious of itself and doesn't have a voice. So no one can discover this treasure store. It is just the same with beings. But there is nothing that the power of the Tathagata's vision is afraid of. The treasure store of the great dharma is within beings' bodies. It does not hear and it is not aware of the addictions and delusions of the five desires (sight, sound, scent, flavor, touch)

Tathagata-garbha Sutra It is like the pit inside amra fruit which does not decay. When you plant it in the ground, it grows into the largest and most regal of trees.

Tathagata-garbha Sutra It is like a man with a statue of pure gold, who was to travel through the narrow roads of another country and feared that he might be victimized and robbed. So he wrapped the statue in worn-out rags so that no one would know that he had it. One day the man suddenly died, and the golden statue was discarded in an open field. Travelers trampled it and it became totally filthy. But a person with supernatural vision saw that within the worn-out rags there was a pure gold statue, so he unwrapped it and paid homage to it.

Tathagata-garbha Sutra It is like a woman who is impoverished, vile, ugly and hated by others, who bears an Arya [royal] son in her womb. He will become a Cakra-vartin [Wheel-turning] King, a ruler of all the four directions. But she does not know his future history and constantly thinks of him as a baseborn, impoverished child.

Tathagata-garbha Sutra It is like a master foundryman casting a statue of pure gold. After casting is complete, it is inverted and placed on the ground. Although the outside is scorched and blackened, the inside is unchanged. When it is opened and the statue taken out, the golden color is radiant and dazzling.

The parable nature of Buddhist teachings fits in with the parable nature of Jesus teachings. The Tathagata-garbha sutra is contemporary with the era of the origins of Christianity. It is evident when reading that Tathagata can at once be read as referring to Buddha, then it can be read as referring to Christ. The dharma can be thought of as the gospel, and it makes perfect sense within either tradition.

Heart Treasure

Matthew 6.21 For where your treasure is, there will your heart be also.

Khandhasamyutta 36 Bhikkhu, if one has an underlying tendency towards something, then one is measured in accordance with it; if one is measured in accordance with something, then one is reckoned in terms of it. If one does not have an underlying tendency towards something, then one is not measured in accordance with it; if one is not measured in accordance with something, then one is not reckoned in terms of it.

The concept of what you treasure being the definition of your heart [Matthew 6.21] goes back to Psalm 119.72 – The law of thy mouth is better to me than thousands of gold and silver.

The way I think about this verse is: The ToWRaH words are more treasured by me than all of the wealth of the world

Tao Te Ching 44 Fame or self: which matters more? Self or wealth: which is more precious? Gain or loss: which is more painful? He who is attached to things will suffer much. He who saves will suffer heavy loss.

Dvedhavitakka Sutta 6 Bhikkhus, whatever a bhikkhu frequently thinks and ponders upon, that will become the inclination of his mind.

Buddha went on to explain in this thread (sutta) that the mind can be inclined towards whatever we select to value, be it renunciation, sensual desire, ill will, or cruelty. Whatever we focus upon is given energy that then pulls us in a particular direction and thus defines us. We can buy into it, energized by all the media and culture at hand, or we can stand aloof from it all. We don't have to be controlled and led around by what we are expected to want and stand for and stand against, we can choose, select what we value, select what drives us and compels us through life.

Corpus Hermeticum 13.14 The visible body born of nature is far different from that of spiritual birth. For the one can be dissolved and the other cannot; the one is mortal and the other immortal. Do you not know that you have become divine and that you are a son of the One? So also am I.

Maitri Upanishad 6.24 If men thought of God as much as they think of the world, who would not attain liberation?

Vision

Matthew 6.22 The light of the body is the eye: if therefore thine eye be single, thy whole body shall be full of light.

Matthew 6.23 But if thine eye be evil, thy whole body shall be full of darkness. If therefore the light that is in thee be darkness, how great is that darkness!

Single or evil, focused or distracted, pure vision or a haze of lies?

John 1.4-5 In him was life; and the life was the light of men. And the light shineth in darkness; and the darkness comprehended it not.

Dialogue of the Saviour 8 The lamp of the body is the mind. As long as the things inside you are set in order, [...] your bodies are luminous.

Psalm 19.7-8 The law of the LORD is perfect, converting the soul: the testimony of the LORD is sure, making wise the simple. The statutes of the LORD are right, rejoicing the heart: the commandment of the LORD is pure, enlightening the eyes.

Psalm 119.104-105 Through thy precepts I get understanding: therefore I hate every false way. Thy word is a lamp unto my feet, and a light unto my path.

Deuteronomy 11.18 Therefore shall ye lay up these my words in your heart and in your soul, and bind them for a sign upon your hand, that they may be as frontlets between your eyes.

Ariyapariyesana Sutta 20 Venerable sir, let the Blessed One teach the Dharma, let the Sublime One teach the Dharma. There are beings with little dust in their eyes who are wasting through not hearing the Dharma. There will be those who will understand the Dharma.

Salayatanasamyutta 228 The eye, bhikkhus, is the ocean for a person; its current consists of forms. One who withstands that current consisting of forms is said to have crossed the ocean of the eye with its waves, whirlpools, sharks, and demons. Crossed over, gone beyond, the Brahmin stands on high ground.

The "evil" of the eye is an arising of cravings, a loss of focused purity. While we are not all confined to monastic vows of chastity and poverty, there are other temptation distractions that haunt our visions at times. It could be the cake in view when we intend on being on a diet. It could be the cigarette in view when we intend to quit smoking.

Culasaccaka Sutta 26 The liberated mind possesses three unsurpassable qualities – perfect vision, perfect practice of the way, and perfect deliverance.

Udanavarga 12.2 Just as dust raised by the wind is settled by rain, so misconceptions are settled when one sees with the eyes of wisdom.

Bhagavad Gita 2.41 The follower of this path has one thought, and this is the End of his determination. But many-branched and endless are the thoughts of the man who lacks determination.

Bhagavad Gita 2.69 In the dark night of all beings awakes to Light the tranquil man. But what is day to other beings is night for the sage who sees.

Bhagavad Gita 12.15 He whose peace is not shaken by others, whose soul is in harmony and whose determination is strong; whose mind and inner vision are set on me – this man loves me, and he is dear to me.

You only have to go around a couple of times before it gets so tight that all is one. Your focus keeps you in the same path, on the one circuit, until you arrive at your destination. To see requires to expose. To hear requires to make sound. To touch requires to offer touch. To know requires to be taught and to consider the whole of revelation. What they are impressed to learn are just frustrating pieces to a much larger puzzle that they do not even know they are working on. Either you are helping to solve the puzzle or you are in the way. Either you have found a harmonious determination or you haven't. Focus.

What is Really Ruling over You and Oppressing You?

Matthew 6.24 No man can serve two masters: for either he will hate the one, and love the other; or else he will hold to the one, and despise the other. Ye cannot serve God and mammon.

Mammonas is the Greek word for treasure, riches. If you found yourself as a pirate, you would have to want to serve the quest for treasure to the exclusion of wanting to be a good citizen of the British Empire. You can't be both at the same time. What Jesus is proposing here is that if you are this reverse-pirate, you are seeking allegiance with a spiritual kingdom, and seeking an elusive treasure that makes all the gold you could find seem meaningless in comparison.

Thomas 47 Jesus said, "It is impossible for a man to mount two horses or to stretch two bows. And it is impossible for a servant to serve two masters; otherwise, he will honor the one and treat the other contemptuously. No man drinks old wine and immediately desires to drink new wine. And new wine is not put into old wineskins, lest they burst; nor is old wine put into a new wineskin, lest it spoil it. An old patch is not sewn into a new garment, because a tear would result."

The God beyond the material is contrasted with the "Almighty Dollar" mammon. In the parallel verse, Luke makes it perfectly clear that it was the "prosperity gospel" of the "Pharisees" that was being challenged here by Jesus. Luke then adds two pericopes here (after Luke 16.13). The first makes it clear that Jesus has no concern for who possesses what in a material sense. The second drives home the point that all the material riches collected are worthless from the perspective of the God beyond the material. This getting beyond the material places the spiritual person beyond concerns for politics and who rules what and who owns what.

Pseudo-Phocylides 42-47 The love of money is the mother of all evil. Gold and silver are always a lure for men. Gold, originator of evil, destroyer of life, crushing all things, would that you were not a desirable calamity to mortals! For your sake there are battles and plunderings and murders, and children become the enemies of their parents, and brothers the enemies of their kinsmen.

1 Timothy 6.10 For the love of money is the root of all evil: which while some coveted after, they have erred from the faith, and pierced themselves through with many sorrows.

Apollonius of Tyana 5.36.2 Do not consider what is stored away to be real wealth, since how is that better than sand piled up from anywhere?

Apollonius of Tyana 6.2.2 It was indeed a good time when wealth was in dishonor, equality flourished, dark iron was hidden away because mankind was united, and the whole world was considered one.

Gamanisamyutta 10 The ascetics following the Sakyan son do not accept gold and silver. They have renounced jewellery and gold; they have given up the use of gold and silver.

Tao Te Ching 42 For one gains by losing and loses by gaining.

Ratthapala Sutta 42 I see men wealthy in the world, who yet from ignorance give not their gathered wealth, greedily they hoard away their riches longing still for further sensual pleasures.

Abu 'Abdallah Ahmad b. Muhammad al-Shaybani Ibn Hanbal: Kitab al-Zuhd 310 Jesus said to the disciples, "Truly I say to you, you desire neither this world nor the next." They said, "Prophet of God, explain this matter to us, for we used to think that we desired one of them." He said, "Had you desired this world, you would have obeyed the Lord of the world, who holds the keys of its treasures in His hands. Had you desired the other world, you would have obeyed the Lord who owns it, and He would have given it to you. But you want neither the one nor the other."

Corpus Hermeticum 4.6 It is impossible to be governed by both, by the mortal and by the divine. There are two kinds of beings, the embodied and unembodied, in whom there is the mortal and the divine spirit. Man is left to choose one or the other, if he so wishes. For one cannot choose both at once; when one is diminished, it reveals the power of the other.

Unlearn what you have Prioritized

Matthew 6.25 Therefore I say unto you, Take no thought for your life, what ye shall eat, or what ye shall drink; nor yet for your body, what ye shall put on. Is not the life more than meat, and the body than raiment?

Matthew 6.26 Behold the fowls of the air: for they sow not, neither do they reap, nor gather into barns; yet your heavenly Father feedeth them. Are ye not much better than they?

Matthew 6.27 Which of you by taking thought can add one cubit unto his stature?

Matthew 6.28 And why take ye thought for raiment? Consider the lilies of the field, how they grow; they toil not, neither do they spin:

Matthew 6.29 And yet I say unto you, That even Solomon in all his glory was not arrayed like one of these.

Matthew 6.30 Wherefore, if God so clothe the grass of the field, which to day is, and to morrow is cast into the oven, shall he not much more clothe you, O ye of little faith?

Matthew 6.31 Therefore take no thought, saying, What shall we eat? or, What shall we drink? or, Wherewithal shall we be clothed?

Matthew 6.32 (For after all these things do the Gentiles seek:) for your heavenly Father knoweth that ye have need of all these things.

Udanavarga 2.1-2 O desire, I know your root; it is from imagination that you spring. I will not imagine you, and you will not arise in me. From desires spring grief, from desires spring fear.

Pythagorean / Stoic values. Free from desire. Take no thought. Free as a bird. Natural. This "always concerned" lifestyle is stressing out nearly everyone. Be careless.

Apollonius of Tyana 3.15.1 I saw the Indian Brahmans [holy men of God] living on the earth and not on it, walled without walls, owning nothing and owning everything.

Apollonius of Tyana 3.15.3 Apollonius therefore rightly says that they have what they do not have, since they make no preparations in advance, but obtain everything they want on the spot.

Apollonius of Tyana 7.30.1 My life is an improvisation.

Udanavarga 2.12-13 He who seeks complete happiness, let him renounce all desires; having renounced all desires, he attains supreme happiness. As long as desire is pursued, mental contentment is not found.

Barnabas 19.6 Thou shalt not be found coveting thy neighbor's goods; thou shalt not be found greedy of gain. Neither shalt thou cleave with thy soul to the lofty, but shalt walk with the humble and righteous. The accidents that befall thee thou shalt receive as good, knowing that nothing is done without God. Thou shalt not be double minded nor double tongued.

Didache 3.9-10 Thou shalt not exalt thyself, nor let thy soul be presumptuous. Thy soul shall not consort with the lofty, but thou shalt walk with righteous and humble men. Receive the accidents that befall to thee as good, knowing that nothing happens without God.

Thomas 36 Jesus said, "Do not be concerned from morning until evening and from evening until morning about what you will wear."

Talmud: Sotah 48b Rabbi Eliezer the Great declares: Whoever has a piece of bread in his basket and says. 'What shall I eat tomorrow?' belongs only to them who are little in faith.

Pseudo-Phocylides 116-121 Nobody knows what will be after tomorrow or after an hour. Death is heedless of mortals, and the future is uncertain. Do not let evils dismay you nor therefore exult in success. Many times in life incredible calamity has come suddenly to the confident and release from evil to the vexed. Accommodate yourself to the circumstances, do not blow against the winds.

Lotus Sutra 14 Clothing and bedding, food, drink, medicine – with regards to such things he should have no expectations but with a single mind concentrate upon the reasons for preaching the Law, desiring to complete the Buddha way and to cause those in the assembly to do likewise. That will bring great gain to them, an offering of peace.

Ganaka Moggallana Sutta 5 Come, bhikkhu, be moderate in eating. Reflecting wisely, you should take food neither for amusement nor for intoxication nor for the sake of physical beauty and attractiveness, but only for the endurance and continuance of this body, for ending discomfort, and for assisting the holy life, considering: "Thus I shall terminate old feelings without arousing new feelings and I shall be healthy and blameless and shall live in comfort."

Akankheyya Sutta 7 If a bhikkhu should wish: 'May I become a conqueror of discontent and delight, and may discontent and delight not conquer me; may I abide transcending discontent and delight whenever they arise,' let him fulfil the precepts, be devoted to internal serenity of mind, not neglect meditation, be possessed of insight, and dwell in empty huts.

Vanapattha Sutta 3-4 The bhikkhu should consider thus: 'I am living in this jungle thicket. While I am living here my unestablished mindfulness does not become established, my unconcentrated mind does not become concentrated, my undestroyed taints do not come to destruction, I do not attain the unstained supreme security from bondage; and also the requisites of life that should be obtained by one gone forth – robes, almsfood, resting place, and medicinal requisites – are hard to come by.' That bhikkhu should depart from that jungle thicket that very night or that very day; he should not continue living there.

Buddha thus taught, don't leave yourself in a place where you will wither and die, but prioritize spiritual needs over physical needs. Life can be a jungle, cold and harsh, but life is also a choice, situation a condition of not moving on, circumstance a fluid snapshot of possibilities that can present themselves to anyone free of attachments enough to consider change and letting go. Cut the ties and unlearn the habits.

Bhagavad Gita 2.14-15 From the world of the senses, Arjuna, comes heat and comes cold, and pleasure and pain. They come and they go: they are transient. Arise above them, strong soul. The man whom these cannot move, whose soul is one, beyond pleasure and pain, is worthy of life in Eternity.

Bhagavad Gita 2.56-58 He whose mind is untroubled by sorrows, and for pleasures he has no longings, beyond passion, and fear and anger, he is the sage of unwavering mind. Who everywhere is free from all ties, who neither rejoices nor sorrows if fortune is good or is ill, he is a serene wisdom. When in recollection he withdraws all his senses from the attractions of the pleasures of sense, even as a tortoise withdraws all its limbs, then his is a serene wisdom.

Bhagavad Gita 4.14 In the bonds of works I am free, because in them I am free from desires. The man who can see this truth, in his work he finds his freedom.

Beyond their concerns, what the world seeks, what culture values, what politics and laws allow. What concerns most, what worries most, what occupies most, are things that come and go, that in the end do not matter. Needs are supplied as needed. It all works out. Every crisis will pass. Every hot summer, every freezing winter, every happy accident pleasant window of opportunity, every disaster that arises, will come and go. None of what most, "the world", actually cares about ends up mattering. This same conclusion frames the paradigms of the Buddhist, the Stoic, the monastic of various orders and traditions, the counter-culture "reassess values and challenge the institutions of traditions" movements of revolutionary mindset shifts in values and consciousness. This keeps coming up again and again in human history. The hippies of the 1960s did not invent this mindset that values freedom beyond material gain.

Matthew 10.37 He that loveth father or mother more than me is not worthy of me: and he that loveth son or daughter more than me is not worthy of me.

Who leaves father or mother for me will be rewarded, Christ promises. Withdraw. Check out. Fall off the edge of the world. Drop out. Quit. Vanish. Leave it all behind. Father politics and mother religion are over protecting you and holding you back. Think outside their boxes. Stop being a carrier. Your goal is not to leave behind son politics or daughter religion. Your goal is to break the chain.

AL AN'AM 6.38 There is not an animal (that lives) on the earth, nor a being that flies on its wings, but (forms part of) communities like you. Nothing have we omitted from the Book, and they (all) shall be gathered to their Lord in the end.

AL AN'AM 6.59 With Him are the keys of the unseen, the treasures that none knoweth but He. He knoweth whatever there is on the earth and in the sea. Not a leaf doth fall but with His knowledge: there is not a grain in the darkness (or depths) of the earth, nor anything fresh or dry (green or withered), but is (inscribed) in a record clear (to those who can read).

HUD 11.6 There is no moving creature on earth but its sustenance dependeth on Allah: He knoweth the time and place of its definite abode and its temporary deposit: All is in a clear Record.

AL HAJJ 22.63 Seest thou not that Allah sends down rain from the sky, and forthwith the earth becomes clothed with green? For Allah is He Who understands the finest mysteries, and is well-acquainted (with them).

Providence. Fate. Synchronicity. Synergy of forces beyond explanation. Just in time opportunity. When it always words out, you get over worrying about the specifics of the current crisis at hand. The difference between abject failure and amazing success is but the touch of one serendipitous aha moment. This too shall pass.

AL MULK 67.19 Do they not observe the birds above them, spreading their wings and folding them in? None can uphold them except (Allah) Most Gracious: Truly (Allah) Most Gracious: Truly it is He that watches over all things.

AL NISA' 4.79 Whatever good, (O man!) happens to thee, is from Allah; but whatever evil happens to thee, is from thy (own) soul. And We have sent thee as a messenger to (instruct) mankind. And enough is Allah for a witness.

AL SAFFAT 37.40-41 But the sincere (and devoted) Servants of Allah – for them is a Sustenance determined,

AL A'LA 87.4-5 And Who bringeth out the (green and luscious) pasture, and then doth make it (but) swarthy stubble.

Sit back and watch the waves – spring to fall, birth to death – and keeping surfing them. The only constant is change, and the only way to fall off the wave is to try to be rigid and remain in one place, all secure and prepared. It doesn't work that way; you have to be agile. Wait for the windows of opportunity to present themselves, then jump. Wait for Mercury to appear and then grab him by the short hairs.

AL MA'IDAH 5.114 Said Jesus the son of Mary: "O Allah our Lord! Send us from heaven a table set (with viands), that there may be for us – for the first and the last of us – a solemn festival and a sign from thee; and provide for our sustenance, for thou art the best Sustainer (of our needs)."

'Abdallah al-Marwazi Ibn al-Mubarak: Kitab al-Zuhd wa al-Raqa'iq 627 Jesus said, "For the patient man, misfortune soon results in ease; for the sinner, ease soon results in misfortune."

'Abdallah al-Marwazi Ibn al-Mubarak: Kitab al-Zuhd wa al-Raqa'iq 848
Jesus said, "Strive for the sake of God and not for the sake of your
bellies. Look at the birds coming and going! They neither reap nor
plough, and God provides for them. If you say, 'Our bellies are larger
than the bellies of birds,' then look at the cattle, wild or tame, as they
come and go, neither reaping nor plowing and God provides for them
too. Beware the excesses of the world, for the excesses of the world
are an abomination in God's eyes."

Kingdom of God

**Matthew 6.33 But seek ye first the kingdom of God, and his
righteousness; and all these things shall be added unto you.**

"Of God" is not in the actual Greek original for this verse. The focus to
be sought after is the "kingdom of righteousness". Kingdom is
basileian in Greek, while righteousness is dikaiosunen. Basileian
means the extent of influence, the total area where the effect is evident.
In governments, the edges of the kingdom are the boundaries of the
country. Here, we have a hint that Jesus is not referring to political
boundaries. Dikaiosunen means "as it ought to be", the natural state,
the acceptable approved of state of integrity, virtue, purity, correct, with
justice and righteousness prevailing. Work on building a giant all-
inclusive bubble of peace and harmony and then live within that world.
Extend the inherent order. Focus on the presence of order and it will
all work out for you in the end. The Romans brought soldiers to control
the uprisings of the terrorists, to build roads, aqueducts, education.
What will natural order bring to those who trust in it? What will the
"kingdom not of this world" bring to this world?

Corpus Hermeticum 11.21 When you take that road this Good will
meet you everywhere and will be experienced everywhere, even where
and when you do not expect it; when awake, asleep, in a ship, on the
road, by night, by day, when speaking and when silent, for there is
nothing which it is not.

Apollonius of Tyana 7.13.10 If the intellect makes good choices,
Conscience will escort a true man into every sanctuary, every street,
every sacred enclosure, and every haunt of men, applauding him and
singing his praises. It will sing to him when while he sleeps,
surrounding him with propitious choirs from the commonwealth of
dreams.

Dead Sea Scrolls 4Q473 1.2-5 There are two ways, one good and one evil. If you walk in the good way, He will bless you. But if you walk in the evil way, He will curse you in your going out and in your tents.

You want to resonate with synergy with God. Then everything magically falls in place. You can stop being stressed out. You can trust in the energy from God to arrive, because you have gnosis of your connection. This is beyond having any sense of blind faith or superstition. This is a knowing from direct experience gnosis, like you know what your parents look like, what your children look like, what your spouse looks like. Your connection to God is just this intimate and real to you. This is the gnosis that brings synergy with God.

Proverbs 14.8 The wisdom of the prudent is to understand his way: but the folly of fools is deceit.

The way I think about this verse is: "To those who have discretion, Sophia guards their life path. Those foolish of her find themselves off course."

Romans 8.28 And we know that all things work together for good to them that love God, to them who are the called according to his purpose.

The "work together" is sunergei in Greek, synergy. What if there was a way to be so harmonious that God supported you in your quest for harmony? Wisdom is key. Embrace wisdom. Hold her. Don't let her escape.

Wisdom of Solomon 7.7-8 Wherefore I prayed, and understanding was given me: I called upon God, and the spirit of wisdom came to me. I preferred her before sceptres and thrones, and esteemed riches nothing in comparison of her.

Tomorrow

Matthew 6.34 Take therefore no thought for the morrow: for the morrow shall take thought for the things of itself. Sufficient unto the day is the evil thereof.

Abu 'Abdallah Ahmad b. Muhammad al-Shaybani Ibn Hanbal: Kitab al-Zuhd 488 Jesus used to say, "O disciples, do not seek the world by destroying yourselves; seek your salvation by abandoning what is in the world. Naked you came into the world and naked you shall depart.

Do not seek what sustenance tomorrow may bring, but let each day's sustenance suffice and tomorrow will bring its own concerns. Pray God to bring you sustenance day by day."`

Talmud: Berakoth 9b A parable: They were like a man who was kept in prison and people told him: To-morrow, they will release you from the prison and give you plenty of money. And he answered them: I pray of you, let me go free today and I shall ask nothing more!

Be here now.

Bhaddekaratta Sutta 3 Let not a person revive the past or on the future build his hopes; for the past has been left behind and the future has not been reached. Instead with insight let him see each presently arisen state; let him know that and be sure of it, invincibly, unshakeably. Today the effort must be made; tomorrow Death may come, who knows? No bargain with Mortality can keep him and his hordes away, but one who dwells thus ardently, relentlessly, by day, by night – it is he, the Peaceful Sage has said, who has had a single excellent night [unending excellent Nirvana].

The advice to never worry about tomorrow is given. From Dead Sea Scrolls Damascus Document Geniza A 10.19, "[On the Sabbath day] one may not discuss business or work to be done the next day." Perhaps this was taken a degree further in advising that one never worries about the future. What if every day was considered holy?

AL KAHF 18.23-24 Nor say of anything, "I shall be sure to do so and so tomorrow" – without adding, "So please Allah!" and call thy Lord to mind when thou forgetest, and say, "I hope that my Lord will guide me ever closer (even) than this to the right road."

LUQMAN 31.34 Verily the knowledge of the Hour is with Allah (alone). It is He Who sends down rain, and He Who knows what is in the wombs. Nor does any one know what it is that he will earn on the morrow: Nor does any one know in what land he is to die. Verily with Allah is full knowledge and He is acquainted (with all things).

Give the Benefit of a Doubt

Matthew 7.1 Judge not, that ye be not judged.

Don't desire to rule if you don't like to be ruled over. Don't be so bossy if you don't like being bossed around. You are not the judge of the

spiritual state of others. You don't really know what they've been
through to come to be how they are today. They don't know you, what
you've been through, how to react to you, why you do and say and
think and value as you do. We all have to ride our own horse. We all
have to tend to our own lamp. We all have to draw water from our own
well.

John 7.24 Judge not according to the appearance, but judge righteous
judgment.

John 8.15 Ye judge after the flesh; I judge no man.

Mark 4.24 And he said unto them, Take heed what ye hear: with what
measure ye mete, it shall be measured to you: and unto you that hear
shall more be given.

Psalms of Solomon 4.2-3 Excessive in words, excessive in
appearance about everyone, he who is harsh in words in condemning
sinners at judgment. And his hand is the first one against him as if in
zeal, yet he himself is guilty of a variety of sins and intemperance.

Dhammapada 4.7 Think not of the faults of others, of what they have
done or not done. Think rather of your own sins, of the things you have
done or not done.

AL SHURA 42.37 Those who avoid the greater crimes and shameful
deeds, and, when they are angry even then forgive;

AL NUR 24.38 That Allah may reward them according to the best of
their deeds, and add even more for them out of His Grace: for Allah
doth provide for those whom He will, without measure.

'Abdallah al-Marwazi Ibn al-Mubarak: Kitab al-Zuhd wa al-Raqa'iq 135
Jesus said to his people, "Do not talk much without the mention of God,
lest your hearts brow hard; for the hard heart is far from God, but you
do not know. Do not examine the sins of people as though you were
lords, but examine them, rather, as though you were servants. Men
are of two kinds: the sick and the healthy. Be merciful to the sick and
give thanks to God for health."

Honesty

**Matthew 7.2 For with what judgment ye judge, ye shall be judged:
and with what measure ye mete, it shall be measured to you again.**

AL SHU'ARA 26.181-183 Give just measure, and cause no loss (to others by fraud). And weigh with scales true and upright. And withhold not things justly due to men, nor do evil in the land, working mischief.

AL NISA' 4.58 Allah doth command you to render back your trusts to those to whom they are due; and when ye judge between man and man, that ye judge with justice: Verily how excellent is the teaching which He giveth you! For Allah is He Who heareth and seeth all things.

AL MUTAFFIFIN 83.1-4 Woe to those that deal in fraud, those who, when they have to receive by measure from men, exact full measure, but when they have to give by measure or weight to men, give less than due. Do they not think that they will be called to account?-

Pseudo-Phocylides 14-16 Give a just measure, and an extra full measure of all things is good. Do not make a balance unequal, but weigh honestly. And do not commit perjury, neither ignorantly nor willingly.

Leviticus 25.14 And if thou sell ought unto thy neighbour, or buyest ought of thy neighbour's hand, ye shall not oppress one another:

Leviticus 19.35-36 Ye shall do no unrighteousness in judgment, in meteyard, in weight, or in measure. Just balances, just weights, a just ephah, and a just hin, shall ye have: I am the LORD your God, which brought you out of the land of Egypt.

Deuteronomy 25.13-14 Thou shalt not have in thy bag divers weights, a great and a small. Thou shalt not have in thine house divers measures, a great and a small.

Knock Out your Faults to Clarify your Vision

Matthew 7.3 And why beholdest thou the mote that is in thy brother's eye, but considerest not the beam that is in thine own eye?

Matthew 7.4 Or how wilt thou say to thy brother, Let me pull out the mote out of thine eye; and, behold, a beam is in thine own eye?

Matthew 7.5 Thou hypocrite, first cast out the beam out of thine own eye; and then shalt thou see clearly to cast out the mote out of thy brother's eye.

Vitakkasanthana Sutta 3 Just as a skilled carpenter or his apprentice might knock out, remove, and extract a coarse peg by means of a fine one, so too when a bhikkhu gives attention to some other sign connect with what is wholesome, then any evil unwholesome thoughts connected with desire, with hate, and with delusion are abandoned in him and subside. With the abandoning of them his mind becomes steadied internally, quieted, brought to singleness, and concentrated.

Salayatanasamyutta 90 Bhikkhus, being stirred is a disease, being stirred is a tumour, being stirred is a dart. Therefore, bhikkhus, the Tathagata dwells unstirred, with the dart removed.

Dhammapada 18.18 It is easier to see the faults of others, but difficult to see one's own faults. One shows the faults of others like chaff winnowed in the wind, but one conceals one's own faults as a cunning gambler conceals his dice.

Thomas 26 Jesus said, "You see the mote in your brother's eye, but you do not see the beam in your own eye. When you cast the beam out of your own eye, then you will see clearly to cast the mote from your brother's eye."

Apollonius of Tyana: Letter 89: Apollonius to Satyrus: Most people are defenders of their own faults and prosecutors of other people's.

Apollonius of Tyana 6.35.1 They say that the command "Know yourself" is difficult, but more difficult, it seems to me, is for a wise man to remain unaltered, since he cannot change evil natures for the better unless he has first trained himself not to change.

Mahagopalaka Sutta 6-7 When evil unwholesome states have arisen, a bhikkhu tolerates them; he does not abandon them, remove them, do away with them, and annihilate them. This is how a bhikkhu fails to pick out flies' eggs. How does a bhikkhu fail to dress wounds? Here, on seeing a form with the eye, a bhikkhu grasps at its signs and features. Even though, when he leaves the eye faculty unguarded, evil unwholesome states of covetousness and grief might invade him, he does not practice the way of its restraint, he does not guard the eye faculty, he does not undertake the restraint of the eye faculty.

Buddha explains in this sutra that you have control of the lens, what is coming through the eyes, the focus of life. As any lens can become dirty, infected, unfit for viewing through, so too the eyes can become infected with sensual desires, thoughts of ill will, cruelty, unwholesome states that become the lens through which we look out at the world.

Protect the Sacred from the Profane / Proper Judging

Matthew 7.6 Give not that which is holy unto the dogs, neither cast ye your pearls before swine, lest they trample them under their feet, and turn again and rend you.

Didache 9.3-5 And concerning the broken Bread: "We give thee thanks, our Father, for the life and knowledge which thou didst make known to us through Jesus thy Child. To thee be glory for ever. As this broken bread was scattered upon the mountains, but was brought together and became one, so let thy Church be gathered together from the ends of the earth into thy Kingdom, for thine is the glory and the power through Jesus Christ for ever." But let none eat or drink of your Eucharist except those who have been baptized in the Lord's Name. For concerning this also did the Lord say, "Give not that which is holy to the dogs."

Thomas 93 "Do not give what is holy to dogs, lest they throw them on the dung heap. Do not throw the pearls to swine.""

The same Aramaic word for "holy thing" is also used for nose ring or ear ring. The verse become more poetic in this light: "Hang not earrings on dogs. Offer not pearls to pigs."

Lotus Sutra 3 Those with the shallow understanding of ordinary persons who are deeply attached to the five desires, cannot comprehend it when they hear it. Do not preach it to them. If a person fails to have faith but instead slanders this sutra, immediately he will destroy all the seeds for becoming a Buddha in this world.

Lotus Sutra 10 This sutra is the storehouse of the secret crux of the Buddhas. It must not be distributed or recklessly transmitted to others. It has been guarded by the Buddhas, the World-Honored Ones, and from times past until now has never been openly expounded. And since hatred and jealousy toward this sutra abound even when the Thus Come One is in the world, how much more will this be so after his passing?

Bhagavad Gita 18.67 These things must never be spoken to one who lacks self-discipline, or who has no love, or who does not want to hear or who argues against me.

You have to know who to moderate, who to ban from the list, who to keep away so that the expression of gnosis is not disrupted.

AL NISA' 4.88 Why should ye be divided into two parties about the Hypocrites? Allah hath upset them for their (evil) deeds. Would ye guide those whom Allah hath thrown out of the Way? For those whom Allah hath thrown out of the Way, never shalt thou find the Way.

AL RA'D 13.17 He sends down water from the skies, and the channels flow, each according to its measure: But the torrent bears away to foam that mounts up to the surface. Even so, from that (ore) which they heat in the fire, to make ornaments or utensils therewith, there is a scum likewise. Thus doth Allah (by parables) show forth Truth and Vanity. For the scum disappears like froth cast out; while that which is for the good of mankind remains on the earth. Thus doth Allah set forth parables.

AL HADID 57.13 One Day will the Hypocrites – men and women – say to the Believers: "Wait for us! Let us borrow (a Light) from your Light!" It will be said: "Turn ye back to your rear! Then seek a Light (where ye can)!" So a wall will be put up betwixt them, with a gate therein. Within it will be Mercy throughout, and without it, all alongside, will be (Wrath and) Punishment!

Abu 'Abdallah Ahmad b. Muhammad al-Shaybani Ibn Hanbal: Kitab al-Zuhd 477 Jesus said to his disciples, "O disciples, do not cast pearls before swine, for the swine can do nothing with them. Do not impart wisdom to one who does not desire it, for wisdom is more precious than pearls, and whoever rejects wisdom is worse than a swine."

Not everyone can get it. This sounds elitist and politically incorrect these days. Religion becomes so dumbed down for the masses, it becomes a series of learned ideas to have blind faith in, a series of rituals and words and symbols and prejudices. Not everyone is ready. Not everyone is initiated into being a priest, or a monk, or a nun. Religion is a noun and not a verb, something you have and identify with, but not a career, not a purpose in life. Not everyone is waiting for the next great spiritual aha moment that you so strongly wish you could offer to them. You don't have to judge them, but you also don't have to waste your energy casting your pearls of wisdom at them. Let them be. There will be those who are asking for the spiritual answers, seeking wisdom, knocking on your door or stalking your presence. Feed those who are hungry.

Ask, Seek, Knock

Matthew 7.7 Ask, and it shall be given you; seek, and ye shall find; knock, and it shall be opened unto you:

Matthew 7.8 For every one that asketh receiveth; and he that seeketh findeth; and to him that knocketh it shall be opened.

Matthew 7.9 Or what man is there of you, whom if his son ask bread, will he give him a stone?

Matthew 7.10 Or if he ask a fish, will he give him a serpent?

Matthew 7.11 If ye then, being evil, know how to give good gifts unto your children, how much more shall your Father which is in heaven give good things to them that ask him?

Respond to the questions. Give to the seeker the answers sought. Initiation secrets for insiders is balanced with the offering that everyone can be insiders. Immediately after blocking access to the dogs and swine of the world, there is a free and unconditional altar call. It is not God blocking any people, it is people blocking themselves by running with the dog pack or being aggressive like wild boars. Whomsoever will, but they have to be willing, have to ask, have to seek, have to knock, and have to care. You open your door to anyone who knocks on it. It is to be freely given to those who would value it.

Revelation 22.17 And the Spirit and the bride say, Come. And let him that heareth say, Come. And let him that is athirst come. And whosoever will, let him take the water of life freely.

Twelfth century Old English proverb: You can lead a horse to water, but you can't make him drink.

Pistis Sophia 133 I have not concealed it, but I have announced it clearly, and I have not set the sinners apart, but I have proclaimed it and said to all men, sinners and righteous alike, saying, "Seek, that you may find; knock, that it may be opened to you; for whoever seeks in truth will find, and to the one who knocks it will be opened". For I have said to all men, "You should seek the mysteries of the Light-kingdom which will purify you and make you pure and lead you into the Light."

Thomas 92 Jesus said, "Seek and you will find. Yet, what you asked me about in former times and which I did not tell you then, now I do desire to tell, but you do not inquire about it."

Thomas 94 Jesus said, "He who seeks will find, and he who knocks will be let in."

Thomas 2 Jesus said, "Let him who seeks continue seeking until he finds. When he finds, he will become troubled. When he becomes troubled, he will be astonished, and he will rule over the all."

Apollonius of Tyana 1.12.1 "Introduce me to the god." "Why do you need an introduction," said he, "if you are good? The gods welcome virtuous men without any go-betweens."

Apollonius of Tyana 1.12.1 I am Asclepius's servant and companion. If you too care for virtue, go before the god without fear and make what prayer you want.

Jeremiah 29.12-14 Then shall ye call upon me, and ye shall go and pray unto me, and I will hearken unto you. And ye shall seek me, and find me, when ye shall search for me with all your heart. And I will be found of you, saith the LORD: and I will turn away your captivity, and I will gather you from all the nations, and from all the places whither I have driven you, saith the LORD; and I will bring you again into the place whence I caused you to be carried away captive.

It is symbolic. We have become scattered, diffused, out of focus, pushed around and captivated by the world. We have to want to come home, back to one, back in focus, seek the good and simple way we are meant to be.

Revelation 3.8 I know thy works: behold, I have set before thee an open door, and no man can shut it: for thou hast a little strength, and hast kept my word, and hast not denied my name.

Shepherd of Hermas Mandate 9 1.1-6 He saith to me; "Remove from thyself a doubtful mind and doubt not at all whether to ask of God, saying within thyself, "How can I ask a thing of the Lord and receive it, seeing that I have committed so many sins against Him?" Reason not thus, but turn to the Lord with thy whole heart, and ask of Him nothing wavering, and thou shalt know His exceeding compassion, that He will surely not abandon thee, but will fulfill the petition of thy soul. For God is not as men who bear a grudge, but Himself is without malice and hath compassion on His creatures. Do thou therefore cleanse thy heart

112

from all the vanities of this life, and from the things mentioned before; and ask of the Lord, and thou shalt receive all things, and shalt lack nothing of all thy petitions, if thou ask of the Lord nothing wavering. But if thou waver in thy heart, thou shalt surely receive none of thy petitions. For they that waver towards God, these are the doubtful-minded, and they never obtain any of their petitions. But they that are complete in the faith make all their petitions trusting in the Lord, and they receive, because they ask without wavering, nothing doubting; for every doubtful-minded man, if he repent not, shall hardly be saved.

James 1.6-8 But let him ask in faith, nothing wavering. For he that wavereth is like a wave of the sea driven with the wind and tossed. For let not that man think that he shall receive any thing of the Lord. A double minded man is unstable in all his ways.

As Buddha put it in his Noble Eightfold Path, vision must awaken intention, words, actions, situations, caring, excelling, mastering.

Canki Sutta 22 Striving is most helpful for the final arrival at truth, Bharadvaja. If one does not strive, one will not finally arrive at truth; but because one strives, one does finally arrive at truth. That is why striving is most helpful for the final arrival at truth.

The Law in a Nutshell

Matthew 7.12 Therefore all things whatsoever ye would that men should do to you, do ye even so to them: for this is the law and the prophets.

Matthew 22:36-40 Master, which is the great commandment in the law? Jesus said unto him, Thou shalt love the Lord thy God with all thy heart, and with all thy soul, and with all thy mind. This is the first and great commandment. And the second is like unto it, Thou shalt love thy neighbour as thyself. On these two commandments hang all the law and the prophets.

Didache 1.2 The Way of Life is this: "First, thou shalt love the God who made thee, secondly, thy neighbour as thyself; and whatsoever thou wouldst not have done to thyself, do not thou to another."

Tobit 4.14-16 Let not the wages of any man, which hath wrought for thee, tarry with thee, but give him it out of hand: for if thou serve God, he will also repay thee: be circumspect my son, in all things thou doest, and be wise in all thy conversation. Do that to no man which thou hatest: drink not wine to make thee drunken: neither let drunkenness go with thee in thy journey. Give of thy bread to the hungry, and of thy garments to them that are naked; and according to thine abundance give alms: and let not thine eye be envious, when thou givest alms.

Abu 'Abdallah Ahmad b. Muhammad al-Shaybani Ibn Hanbal: Kitab al-Zuhd 332 A man came to Jesus and said, "Teacher of goodness, teach me something that you know and I do not, that benefits me and does you no harm." Jesus asked, "What would that be?" The man said, "How can a servant be truly pious before God?" Jesus replied, "The matter is easy. You must truly love God in your heart and work in His service, exerting all your effort and strength, and be merciful toward the people of your race as you show mercy to yourself." He said, "Teacher of goodness, who are the people of my race?" Jesus replied, "All the children of Adam. And that which you do not wish done to you, do not do unto others. In this way you will be truly pious before God."

Udanavarga 5.18-19 Travelling mentally in all directions, nowhere does one find an object more beloved than oneself; in the same way, each of the others is dear to himself; thus, one should not do wrong to another to satisfy oneself. Everyone fears violence, everyone loves life; be an example and abstain from killing or causing killing.

Put yourself in the position of whoever you find yourself angry with.

Alternate Routes

Matthew 7.13 Enter ye in at the strait gate: for wide is the gate, and broad is the way, that leadeth to destruction, and many there be which go in thereat:

Matthew 7.14 Because strait is the gate, and narrow is the way, which leadeth unto life, and few there be that find it.

The popular way led many to violent revolution and death. Destroyed temple. Jerusalem lost. Dreams burnt in piles of rubble. The unpopular alternative is the way of peace. Peace can be unpatriotic. Peace can be godless. Peace threatens their goals, their values, and their religious fanaticism. Not a popular position when war is the immanent mindset of the masses.

Didache 1.1 There are two Ways, one of Life and one of Death, and there is a great difference between the two Ways.

AL HAJJ 22.54 And that those on whom knowledge has been bestowed may learn that the (Qur'an) is the Truth from thy Lord, and that they may believe therein, and their hearts may be made humbly (open) to it: for verily Allah is the Guide of those who believe, to the Straight Way.

The Straight Way is an interesting term. While Muhammad sought out the Direct Path to the Oneness of God, and Gautama sought out the Smoothest Path to the Awakening [Buddha] of the Oneness [Nirvana], it seems Jesus sought out the Narrowest Path to the Oneness of God, the narrowness ensuring a more accurate hitting of the bull's eye mark. I suppose it make be argued that saying the most Direct of Paths would by definition fall within the Narrowest of Paths that reaches the same Goal. The straight thus is the narrow, the strait.

Barnabas 18.1-2 But let us pass on to another lesson and teaching. There are two ways of teaching and of power, the one of light and the other of darkness; and there is a great difference between the two ways. For on the one are stationed the light giving angels of God, on the other the angels of Satan. And the one is the Lord from all eternity and unto all eternity, whereas the other is Lord of the season of iniquity that now is.

Shepherd of Hermas Mandate 6 1.2-4 Do thou therefore trust righteousness, but trust not unrighteousness; for the way of righteousness is straight, but the way of unrighteousness is crooked. But walk thou in the straight and level path, and leave the crooked one alone. For the crooked way has no tracks, but only pathlessness and many stumbling stones, and is rough and thorny. So it is therefore harmful to those who walk in it. But those who walk in the straight way walk on the level and without stumbling: for it is neither rough nor thorny. Thou seest then that it is more expedient to walk in this way."

Dead Sea Scrolls Community Rule 1QS 5.10-12 Each one who thus enters the Covenant by oath is to separate from all of the perverse men, they who walk in the wicked way, for such are not reckoned a part of His Covenant. They "have not sought Him nor inquired of His statutes" so as to discover the hidden laws in which they err to their shame. Even the revealed laws they knowingly transgress.

Shepherd of Hermas Mandate 6 2.3-4 "Hear," saith he, "and understand their workings. The angel of righteousness is delicate and bashful and gentle and tranquil. When then this one enters into thy heart, forthwith he speaketh with thee of righteousness, of purity, of holiness, and of contentment, of every righteous deed and of every glorious virtue. When all these things enter into thy heart, know that the angel of righteousness is with thee. These then are the works of the angel of righteousness. Trust him therefore and his works. Now see the works of the angel of wickedness also. First of all, he is quick tempered and bitter and senseless, and his works are evil, overthrowing the servants of God. Whenever then he entereth into thy heart, know him by his works."

Deuteronomy 30.19 I call heaven and earth to record this day against you, that I have set before you life and death, blessing and cursing: therefore choose life, that both thou and thy seed may live.

Jeremiah 21.8 And unto this people thou shalt say, Thus saith the LORD; Behold, I set before you the way of life, and the way of death.

Jeremiah 6.16 Stand at the corner and observe, asking for the old and narrow path. Take that path and find rest for your souls. But they said they would not take that path.

1 Enoch 91.3-4 Then he [Enoch] spoke to all of them, children of righteousness, and said, "Hear, all you children of Enoch, the talk of your father and listen to my voice in uprightness; for I exhort you, my beloved, and say to you: Love uprightness, and it alone. Do not draw near uprightness with an ambivalent attitude, and neither associate with hypocrites. But walk in righteousness, my children, and it shall lead you in the good paths; and righteousness shall be your friend.

1 Enoch 91.18-19 Now I shall speak unto you, my children, and show you the ways of righteousness and the ways of wickedness. Moreover, I shall make a revelation to you so that you may know that which is going to take place. Now listen to me, my children, and walk in the way of righteousness, and do not walk in the way of wickedness, for all those who walk in the ways of injustice shall perish."

1 Enoch 94.1-4 "Now, my children, I say to you: Love righteousness and walk therein! For the ways of righteousness are worthy of being embraced, but the ways of wickedness shall soon perish and diminish. To certain known persons, the ways of injustice and death shall be revealed as soon as they are born; and they shall keep themselves at a distance from those ways and would not follow them. Now to you, those righteous ones, I say: Do not walk in the evil way, or in the way of death! Do not draw near to them lest you be destroyed! But seek for yourselves and choose righteousness and the elect life! Walk in the way of peace so that you shall have life and be worthy!

2 Esdras 7.3-5 And I said, Speak on, my God. Then said he unto me, The sea is set in a wide place, that it might be deep and great. But put the case the entrance were narrow, and like a river; who then could go into the sea to look upon it, and to rule it? If he went not through the narrow, how could he come into the broad?

2 Esdras 7.12 then were the entrances of this world made narrow, full of sorrow and travail: they are but few and evil, full of perils, and very painful.

Sometimes you have to take the alternative route to get out of the traffic jam of common culture and reach your destination.

Corpus Hermeticum 12.23 There is one way to worship God: be not evil.

Dvedhavitakka Sutta 25 Suppose, bhikkhus, that in a wooded range there was a great low-lying marsh near which a large herd of deer lived. Then a man appeared desiring their ruin, harm, and bondage, and he closed off the safe and good path that led to their happiness, and he opened up a false path, and he put out a decoy and set up a dummy so that the large herd of deer might later come upon calamity, disaster, and loss. But another man came desiring their good, welfare, and protection, and he reopened the safe and good path that led to their happiness, and he closed off the false path, and he removed the decoy and destroyed the dummy, so that the large herd of deer might later come to growth, increase, and fulfilment.

You have been tricked. Unlearn the wrong path and get back on the right track.

Devatasamyutta 46 Resounding with a host of nymphs, haunted by a host of demons! This grove is to be called 'Deluding': how does one escape from it? 'The straight way' that path is called, and 'fearless' is its destination. The chariot is called 'unrattling,' fitted with wheels of wholesome states. The sense of shame is its leaning board, mindfulness its upholstery; I call the Dharma the charioteer, with right view running out in front. One who has such a vehicle – whether a woman or a man – has, by means of this vehicle, drawn close to Nirvana.

Sallekha Sutta 14 Cunda, suppose there were an uneven path and another even path by which to avoid it; and suppose there were an uneven ford and another even ford by which to avoid it.

Devaputtasamyutta 6 Though the path is impassable and uneven, the noble ones walk it, Kamada. The ignoble ones fall down head first, right there on the uneven path, but the path of the noble ones is even, for the noble are even amidst the uneven.

It's all in the mind. Inner peace can be present in the midst of chaos. Reality is mostly subjective.

Satipatthana Sutta 2 Bhikkhus, this is the direct path for the purification of beings, for the surmounting of sorrow and lamentation, for the disappearance of pain and grief, for the attainment of the true way, for the realization of Nirvana.

Bhagavad Gita 15.4-6 But let the wise see, and with the strong sword of dispassion let him cut this strong-rooted tree, and seek that path wherefrom those who go never return. Such a man can say. 'I go for refuge to that Eternal Spirit from whom the stream of creation came at the beginning.' Because the man of pure vision, without pride or delusion, in liberty from the chains of attachments, with his soul ever in his inner Spirit, all selfish desires gone, and free from the two contraries known as pleasure and pain, goes to the abode of Eternity. There the sun shines not, nor the moon gives light, nor fire burns, for the Light of my glory is there. Those who reach that abode return no more.

Bhagavad Gita 2.40 No step is lost on this path, and no dangers are found. And even a little progress is freedom from fear.

Narrow path, narrow gate, one thought: focus. Synchronicity happens to those in such a mindset. It all tends to work out. Needs are supplied as needed. Discernment. Wise choice. New direction. New goal. New values. New definition of truth.

AL FATIHAH 1.6 Show us the straight way,

AL NISA' 4.68 And We should have shown them the Straight Way.

AL FATH 48.2 That Allah may forgive thee thy faults of the past and those to follow; fulfil His favour to thee; and guide thee on the Straight Way;

AL ZUKHRUF 43.43 So hold thou fast to the Revelation sent down to thee; verily thou art on a Straight Way.

AL MU'MINUN 23.73 But verily thou callest them to the Straight Way;

YA SIN 36.61 "And that ye should worship Me, (for that) this was the Straight Way?

TA HA 20.135 Say: "Each one (of us) is waiting: wait ye, therefore, and soon shall ye know who it is that is on the straight and even way, and who it is that has received Guidance."

AL BALAD 90.10-12 And shown him the two highways? But he hath made no haste on the path that is steep. And what will explain to thee the path that is steep?-

Katha Upanishad 3 Awake, arise! Strive for the Highest, and be in the Light! Sages say the path is narrow and difficult to tread, narrow as the edge of a razor.

Chandogya Upanishad 8.4.1 There is a bridge between time and Eternity; and this bridge is Atman, the Spirit of man. Neither day nor night cross that bridge, nor old age, nor death nor sorrow. Evil or sin cannot cross that bridge, because the world of the Spirit is pure. This is why when this bridge has been crossed, the eyes of the blind can see, the wounds of the wounded are healed, and the sick man becomes whole from his sickness. To one who goes over that bridge, the night becomes like unto day; because in the worlds of the Spirit there is a Light which is everlasting.

Apollonius of Tyana 1.7.3 When [Apollonius] reached fifteen he aspired to Pythagoras's way of life, to which some higher power gave him wings to climb..."You live your own way," he said, "and I will live Pythagoras's way."

In how many different ways in different cultures and in different ages have those few with vision been able to see past the culture around them to a better set of values?

Beware False Prophets

Matthew 7.15 Beware of false prophets, which come to you in sheep's clothing, but inwardly they are ravening wolves.

Matthew 24.11-12 And many false prophets shall rise, and shall deceive many. And because iniquity shall abound, the love of many shall wax cold.

Religion without compassion, without integrity, is in the way.

Because the way is narrow, you may think you need a guide. You look to preachers and web sites and books and workshops, movements, bandwagons to hop onto. Be careful. Don't substitute what is real gnosis for blind faith in dogmatic assertions of those who just want to control your mindset.

Those who seemed to speak for God rallied support for such violence, resulting in so much destruction. They were responsible for arranging rebellions, revolutions, crusades, inquisitions, witch hunts. These hypocrite players of the part of representing God to humanity have corrupted this planet from ancient Messianic pretenders to modern deluded televangelists.

Mark 13.22 For false Christs and false prophets shall rise, and shall shew signs and wonders, to seduce, if it were possible, even the elect.

Dhammapada 26.12 Of what use is your tangled hair, foolish man, of what use your antelope garment, if within you have tangled cravings, and without ascetic ornaments?

AL BAQARAH 2.79 Then woe to those who write the Book with their own hands, and then say: "This is from Allah," to traffic with it for miserable price! – Woe to them for what their hands do write, and for the gain they make thereby.

There is lots of profit in religion, lots of manipulative greedy egocentric control freaks fleecing the flocks. Prosperity gospels miss the whole heart of the Sermon on the Mount. There are xenophobic hate gospels that define "Christianity" to some. There have been false portraits of Christ for centuries, false definitions of what the Gospel should stand for. These false visions sent many on witch hunts and crusades, supported inquisitions, pogroms, condoning slavery, condoning bigotry, with the "Manifest Destiny" to take "heathen" lands, all in the name and vision of some false portrait of "Christ".

Know Them by Their Fruits

Matthew 7.16 Ye shall know them by their fruits. Do men gather grapes of thorns, or figs of thistles?

Matthew 7.17 Even so every good tree bringeth forth good fruit; but a corrupt tree bringeth forth evil fruit.

Matthew 7.18 A good tree cannot bring forth evil fruit, neither can a corrupt tree bring forth good fruit.

Matthew 7.19 Every tree that bringeth not forth good fruit is hewn down, and cast into the fire.

Matthew 7.20 Wherefore by their fruits ye shall know them.

If the Jewish revolutionaries were right, then wouldn't God have backed them up? Wouldn't the Jews have conquered Rome instead of the Romans having conquered Jerusalem? The proof is in the pudding [seventeenth century saying]. They failed, therefore, they were fakes. Or they failed because they were wrong in their assertion that God takes sides in religious concept spawned wars.

Matthew 12.33-35 Either make the tree good, and his fruit good; or else make the tree corrupt, and his fruit corrupt: for the tree is known by his fruit. O generation of vipers, how can ye, being evil, speak good things? For out of the abundance of the heart the mouth speaketh. A good man out of the good treasure of the heart bringeth forth good things: and an evil man out of the evil treasure bringeth forth evil things.

John 6.66 From that time many of his disciples went back, and walked no more with him.

Jesus didn't offer a free ride, but instructions on how to be fruitful in a spiritual endeavor.

Shepherd of Hermas Parable 4 1.5 Do thou therefore bear fruit, that in that summer thy fruit may be known. But abstain from overmuch business, and thou shalt never fall into any sin. For they that busy themselves overmuch, sin much also, being distracted about their business, and in no wise serving their own Lord.

Shepherd of Hermas Parable 3 1.2-3 "Wherefore then, Sir," say I, "are they as if they were withered, and alike?" "Because," saith he, "neither the righteous are distinguishable, nor the sinners in this world, but they are alike. For this world is winter to the righteous, and they are not distinguishable, as they dwell with the sinners. For as in the winter the trees, having shed their leaves, are alike, and are not distinguishable, which are withered, and which alive, so also in this world neither the just nor the sinners are distinguishable, but they are all alike."

Thomas 45 Jesus said, "Grapes are not harvested from thorns, nor are figs gathered from thistles, for they do not produce fruit. A good man brings forth good from his storehouse; an evil man brings forth evil things from his evil storehouse, which is in the heart, and says evil things. For out of the abundance of the heart he brings forth evil things."

Sirach 27.6 The fruit declareth if the tree have been dressed; so is the utterance of a conceit in the heart of man.

2 Esdras 9.17 And he answered me, saying, Like as the field is, so is also the seed; as the flowers be, such are the colours also; such as the workman is, such also is the work; and as the husbandman is himself, so is his husbandry also: for it was the time of the world.

Bhagavad Gita 17.3-4 The faith of a man follows his nature, Arjuna. Man is made of faith: as his faith is so is he. Men of light worship the gods of Light; men of fire worship the gods of power and wealth; men of darkness worship ghosts and spirits of night.

People are either mainly envisioning how they can make their lives better in daytime pursuits of work and interactions, or they are out to conquer their world, or they are out to take what they can from their addictions and cravings. It is only human to be a mixture of the three, productive, ambitious, and self-indulgent. It is a matter of what we allow to take priority in our lives, what we are attached to and what we are detached from. Wealth leads to greed with attachment. Pleasure leads to lust with attachment. Without attachment, the luxuries of life and the pleasures of companionship can be partaken of without destroying the core values possessed by the spiritually minded. It is a narrow tightrope of balance indeed.

Bhagavad Gita 17.14-16 Reverence for the gods of Light, for the twice-born, for the teachers of the Spirit and for the wise; and also purity, righteousness, chastity and non-violence: this is the harmony of the body. Words which give peace, words which are good and beautiful and true, and also the reading of sacred books: this is the harmony of words. Quietness of mind, silence, self-harmony, loving-kindness, and a pure heart: this is the harmony of the mind.

You are the collection of what you value. What are you living for? What stuff do you want to collect? What do you want to accomplish? What do you represent when you are authentically being your true self? It will be evident in your words and actions and reactions and insistences on things being a certain way. By a life virtue driven. By words justified, by words condemned. By that which is heartfelt of a good nature. The gnosis is evident. The tree has ripe fruits.

AL BAQARAH 2.281 And fear the Day when ye shall be brought back to Allah. Then shall every soul be paid what it earned, and none shall be dealt with unjustly.

Judged by one's fruits, without any unjust considerations added in, as bright as one shines, as strong of a foundation as one builds, as perfect as one aspires to be. When God takes a bite of the ripened fruit of your life, will he relish the taste or spit it out? So too, when you consider a spiritual teacher, take a bite of their mindset. Is it sweet and pure, or bitter and judgmental?

AL 'IMRAN 3.25 But how (will they fare) when we gather them together against a day about which there is no doubt, and each soul will be paid out just what it has earned, without (favour or) injustice?

But what about faith in Jesus? Doesn't that stand against being judged by actions, by what you present to the world as your evident spiritual level? Consider what Jesus is saying here next.

AL BAQARAH 2.286 On no soul doth Allah place a burden greater than it can bear. It gets every good that it earns, and it suffers every ill that it earns. (Pray:) "Our Lord! Condemn us not if we forget or fall into error; our Lord! Lay not on us a burden like that which Thou didst lay on those before us; Our Lord! Lay not on us a burden greater than we have strength to bear. Blot out our sins, and grant us forgiveness. Have mercy on us. Thou art our Protector; Help us against those who stand against faith."

Actions Speak Louder Than Words

Matthew 7.21 Not every one that saith unto me, Lord, Lord, shall enter into the kingdom of heaven; but he that doeth the will of my Father which is in heaven.

Matthew 7.22 Many will say to me in that day, Lord, Lord, have we not prophesied in thy name? and in thy name have cast out devils? and in thy name done many wonderful works?

Matthew 7.23 And then will I profess unto them, I never knew you: depart from me, ye that work iniquity.

Culakammavibhanga Sutta 4 Student, beings are owners of their actions, heirs of their actions; they originate from their actions, are bound to their actions, have their actions as their refuge. It is action that distinguishes beings as inferior and superior.

Satipatthanasamyutta 3 It is in just such a way that some foolish persons here make requests of me, but when the Dharma has been spoken to them, they think only of following me around.

Worship Jesus. Worship Krishna Even Buddha caught this sense of being idolized instead of being listened to. Muhammad made it clear, he was a prophet and the focus was to be on Allah and not on himself. Jesus seems to find himself in the same position here. He pushes back: stop idolizing me, stop following me around, take my words and do what I instruct to get yourselves right with God.

Shepherd of Hermas Mandate 7 1.5 "Wherefore, Sir," say I, "didst thou say concerning those that keep His commandments, "They shall live unto God"?" "Because," saith he, "every creature feareth the Lord, but not every one keepeth His commandments. Those then that fear Him and keep His commandments, they have life unto God; but they that keep not His commandments have no life in them."

Shepherd of Hermas Parable 10 4.4 Do therefore good works, whoever of you have received benefits from the Lord, lest, while ye delay to do them, the building of the tower be completed. For it is on your account that the work of the building has been interrupted. Unless then ye hasten to do right, the tower will be completed, and ye shut out."

Apollonius of Tyana: Letter 26: To the cult personnel of Olympia: The gods do not need sacrifices, so what might one do to please them? Acquire wisdom, it seems to me, and do all the good in one's power to those humans who deserve it. That is what pleases the gods, but your actions are those of atheists.

Galatians 6.7 Be not deceived; God is not mocked: for whatsoever a man soweth, that shall he also reap.

Karma. Even from a source that could be labeled by the term "justification by faith", karma is understood. You can only harvest what you have planted.

AL AN'AM 6.120 Eschew all sin, open or secret: those who earn sin will get due recompense for their "earnings."

AL MA'IDAH 5.89 Allah will not call you to account for what is futile in your oaths, but He will call you to account for your deliberate oaths: for expiation, feed ten indigent persons, on a scale of the average for the food of your families; or clothe them; or give a slave his freedom. If that is beyond your means, fast for three days. That is the expiation for the oaths ye have sworn. But keep to your oaths. Thus doth Allah make clear to you His signs, that ye may be grateful.

AL MUNAFIQUN 63.10 And spend something (in charity) out of the substance which We have bestowed on you, before Death should come to any of you and he should say, "O my Lord! Why didst Thou not give me respite for a little while? I should then have given (largely) in charity, and I should have been one of the doers of good".

AL TAGHABUN 64.10 But those who reject Faith and treat Our Signs as falsehoods, they will be Companions of the Fire, to dwell therein for aye: and evil is that Goal.

AL HAQQAH 69.19 Then he that will be given his Record in his right hand will say: "Ah here! Read ye my Record!

AL HAQQAH 69.25 And he that will be given his Record in his left hand, will say: "Ah! Would that my Record had not been given to me!

Matthew 25.31-46 When the Son of man shall come in his glory, and all the holy angels with him, then shall he sit upon the throne of his glory: And before him shall be gathered all nations: and he shall separate them one from another, as a shepherd divideth his sheep from the goats: And he shall set the sheep on his right hand, but the goats on the left. Then shall the King say unto them on his right hand, Come, ye blessed of my Father, inherit the kingdom prepared for you from the foundation of the world: For I was an hungred, and ye gave me meat: I was thirsty, and ye gave me drink: I was a stranger, and ye took me in: Naked, and ye clothed me: I was sick, and ye visited me: I was in prison, and ye came unto me. Then shall the righteous answer him, saying, Lord, when saw we thee an hungred, and fed thee? or thirsty, and gave thee drink? When saw we thee a stranger, and took thee in? or naked, and clothed thee? Or when saw we thee sick, or in prison, and came unto thee? And the King shall answer and say unto them, Verily I say unto you, Inasmuch as ye have done it unto one of the least of these my brethren, ye have done it unto me. Then shall he say also unto them on the left hand, Depart from me, ye cursed, into everlasting fire, prepared for the devil and his angels: For I was an hungred, and ye gave me no meat: I was thirsty, and ye gave me no drink: I was a stranger, and ye took me not in: naked, and ye clothed me not: sick, and in prison, and ye visited me not. Then shall they also answer him, saying, Lord, when saw we thee an hungred, or athirst, or a stranger, or naked, or sick, or in prison, and did not minister unto thee? Then shall he answer them, saying, Verily I say unto you, Inasmuch as ye did it not to one of the least of these, ye did it not to me. And these shall go away into everlasting punishment: but the righteous into life eternal.

Maggasamyutta 34 Few are those among humankind who go beyond to the far shore. The rest of the people merely run up and down along the bank.

I have considered that most people don't want to be spiritually advanced any more than they want to learn how to repair cars or computers or learn to fly a plane. They are happy with superficial religion. Tell them they are saved and let them sing a few songs and then leave. They are satisfied with that. They don't want to be saints. They are actually proud to label themselves as sinners saved by grace. This mindset short-circuits pursuit of sanctification.

Ganaka Moggallana Sutta So too, Brahmin, Nirvana exists and the path leading to Nirvana exists and I am present as the guide. Yet when my disciples have been thus advised and instructed by me, some of them attain Nirvana, the ultimate goal, and some do not attain it. What can I do about that, Brahmin? The Tathagata is one who shows the way.

No one, not Buddha, not Christ, not Muhammad, can force anyone to get it. Everyone has to accept the path and follow the path, and no one can do it for anyone else. They show the way, point the direction, but when people stop to worship the finger instead of walking to where the finger is pointed, they have literally missed the whole point.

AL NISA' 4.123-124 Not your desires, nor those of the People of the Book (can prevail): whoever works evil, will be requited accordingly. Nor will he find, besides Allah, any protector or helper. If any do deeds of righteousness – be they male or female – and have faith, they will enter Heaven, and not the least injustice will be done to them.

FATIR 35.18 Nor can a bearer of burdens bear another's burdens if one heavily laden should call another to (bear) his load. Not the least portion of it can be carried (by the other). Even though he be nearly related. Thou canst but admonish such as fear their Lord unseen and establish regular Prayer. And whoever purifies himself does so for the benefit of his own soul; and the destination (of all) is to Allah.

AL HADID 57.14-15 (Those without) will call out, "Were we not with you?" (The others) will reply, "True! But ye led yourselves into temptation; ye looked forward (to our ruin); ye doubted (Allah's Promise); and (your false) desires deceived you; until there issued the Command of Allah. And the Deceiver deceived you in respect of Allah. "This Day shall no ransom be accepted of you, nor of those who rejected Allah." Your abode is the Fire: that is the proper place to claim you: and an evil refuge it is!"

Depart from me! Gehenna is "hell" in the gospel texts. It means fire pit to burn garbage. Once the dream is in the play, those who cannot share the dream are excluded. Once the parts are assembled to create the whole, the leftover parts are discarded. Be useful and be promoted; be useless and be laid off.

AL MUMTAHINAH 60.3 Of no profit to you will be your relatives and your children on the Day of Judgment: He will judge between you: for Allah sees well all that ye do.

AL MUDDATHTHIR 74.42-46 "What led you into Hell Fire?" They will say: "We were not of those who prayed; "Nor were we of those who fed the indigent; "But we used to talk vanities with vain talkers; "And we used to deny the Day of Judgment,

AL NAML 27.52 Now such were their houses, – in utter ruin, – because they practised wrong-doing. Verily in this is a Sign for people of knowledge.

AL ZUMAR 39.18 Those who listen to the Word, and follow the best (meaning) in it: those are the ones whom Allah has guided, and those are the ones endued with understanding.

MUHAMMAD 47.7-8 O ye who believe! If ye will aid (the cause of) Allah, He will aid you, and plant your feet firmly. But those who reject (Allah) – for them is destruction, and (Allah) will render their deeds astray (from their mark).

This is the key to synergy. We can notice the synchronicity at play, the happy accidents, the events lining up and playing out in our lives as if by magic. What we may not notice is our role in the sequences of opportunities, the changing of minds and situations to aid our very lives, and how this energy draws upon our own will, our own sincerity, our own state of being aligned with greater purposes. This is where synergy comes into play. We can join a group, go to meetings, perform our role and because of our participation see our effect in the end result of the project. We do this in school, at work, in driving in traffic, in many aspects of our lives. What we are talking about is when we have synergy with God, when our wills are amplified by the forces of spiritual energies that come to assist us in our quests. Finding this synergy connection is the key to magic, the key to miracles.

MUHAMMAD 47.11 That is because Allah is the Protector of those who believe, but those who reject Allah have no protector.

Time to Stop Talking and Start Building a YeSoWD (Foundation)

Matthew 7.24 Therefore whosoever heareth these sayings of mine, and doeth them, I will liken him unto a wise man, which built his house upon a rock:

Matthew 7.25 And the rain descended, and the floods came, and the winds blew, and beat upon that house; and it fell not: for it was founded upon a rock.

Matthew 7.26 And every one that heareth these sayings of mine, and doeth them not, shall be likened unto a foolish man, which built his house upon the sand:

Matthew 7.27 And the rain descended, and the floods came, and the winds blew, and beat upon that house; and it fell: and great was the fall of it.

James 2.26 For as the body without the spirit is dead, so faith without works is dead also.

Habakkuk 3.13 Thou wentest forth for the salvation of thy people, even for salvation with thine anointed; thou woundest the head out of the house of the wicked, by discovering the foundation unto the neck. Selah.

YeSoWD is foundation. It is one of those Kabbalah terms. Everyone is trying to build their own YeSoWD, their own little internal spiritual empire. God warned that the wicked could have their covers blown, leaving their YeSoWD vulnerable to decay and attack. The foundational base of physical life is not eternal. We have to find something more substantial to build our houses upon. The symbolism of "Salvation Anointed", of "YeSHuWaH MeSHiYaCH", of "Jesus Christ", coming to the earthly YeSoWD, the Jerusalem temple, and opposing its corrupted state is at play in this verse. The foundation upon the spiritual rock which Jesus offers is contrasted with the stone walled temple which was to be destroyed and abandoned. What is the shell of a dead religion, the fundamentalist cherished faith that has no modern purpose, relics of a different age, no longer living in the hearts of the spiritually alive in the modern world? The gospel of Jesus was revolutionary. The Jerusalem temple was fallen, its less than solid foundation exposed. Christianity spawned in the aftermath, envisioning the building of a spiritual temple not made by human hands in a New Jerusalem not found by physically travelling.

Job 4.18-19 Behold he put no trust in his servants; and his angels he charged with folly: how much less in them that dwell in houses of clay, whose foundation is in the dust, which are crushed before the moth?

Houses are but crumbling clay when the YeSoWD is dust. Like Jesus instructed, don't make your YeSoWD on sand, but make your YeSoWD on rock. Then you protect your YeSoWD, preserve your essence, and keep your authenticity. [Matthew 7.24-27]

Psalm 31.2-3 Bow down thine ear to me; deliver me speedily: be thou my strong rock, for an house of defence to save me. For thou art my rock and my fortress, therefore for thy name's sake lead me, and guide me.

Proverbs 20.27-28 The spirit of man is the candle of the LORD, searching all the inward parts of the belly. Mercy and truth preserve the king: and his throne is upholden by mercy.

The way I think about these verses is: "The spirit [NeSHaMaH] within each of us is the light of God shining through our dark material forms. Mercy [CHeSeD] and a foundation of truth protect the king, whose honor resides in mercy [CHeSeD]."

In these verses from Proverbs we find the themes of inner candle light and a brought forth lovingkindness [CHeSeD] being a foundation for one's throne. These become bookends for the Sermon on the Mount. It begins with tending to light and ends with having built on a foundation that will survive any storm.

Dhammapada 1.13-14 Even as rain breaks through an ill-thatched house, passions will break through an ill-guarded mind. But even as rain breaks not through a well-thatched house, passions break not through a well-guarded mind.

Dead Sea Scrolls 4Q424 1.3-4 A man, when he chooses to build a partition, and he coats the wall with plaster, also he covers it with a roof, otherwise it will fall apart during a downpour.

Your roof is your set of values, your truths, your dharma, your gospel, your tao, your guiding principles.

Bhagavad Gita 2.62-63 When a man dwells on the pleasures of sense, attraction for them arises in him. From attraction arises desire, the lust of possession, and this leads to passion, to anger. From passion comes confusion of mind, then loss of remembrance, the forgetting of duty. From this loss comes the ruin of reason, and the ruin of reason leads man to destruction.

You can crumble your own foundation by being obsessive.

Bhagavad Gita 2.64-65 But the soul that moves in the world of the senses and yet keeps the senses in harmony, free from attraction and aversion, finds rest in quietness. In this quietness falls down the burden of all her sorrows, for when the heart has found quietness, wisdom has also found peace.

Bhagavad Gita 3.31-32 Those who ever follow my doctrine and who have faith, and have a good will, find through pure work their freedom. But those who follow not my doctrine, and who have ill-will, are men blind to all wisdom, confused in mind: they are lost.

Bhagavad Gita 4.20-22 In whatever work he does such a man in truth has peace: he expects nothing, he relies on nothing and ever has fullness of joy. He has no vain hopes, he is the master of his soul, he surrenders all he has, only his body works: he is free from sin. He is glad with whatever God gives him, and he has risen beyond the two contraries here below; he is without jealousy, and in success or in failure he is one: his works bind him not.

Bhagavad Gita 6.36 When the mind is not in harmony, this divine communion is hard to attain; but the man whose mind is in harmony attains it, if he knows and if he strives.

Bhagavad Gita 18.58 If thy soul finds rest in me, thou shalt overcome all dangers by my grace; but if thy thoughts are on thyself, and thou wilt not listen, thou shalt perish.

Abu 'Abdallah Ahmad b. Muhammad al-Shaybani Ibn Hanbal: Kitab al-Zuhd 327 Jesus said, "It is of no use to you to come to know what you

130

did not know, so long as you do not act in accordance with what you already know. Too much knowledge only increases pride if you do not act in accordance with it."

Abu 'Abdallah Ahmad b. Muhammad al-Shaybani Ibn Hanbal: Kitab al-Zuhd 330 Christ said, "Whoever has learned, acted, and imparted knowledge – he is the one who is called great in the kingdom of heaven."

Maitri Upanishad 6.19 There is something beyond our mind which abides in silence within our mind. It is the supreme mystery beyond thought. Let one's mind and one's subtle body rest upon that and not rest on anything else.

The end result: seated in a home on a strong foundation, with a bright light shining while outside there is a dark storm blowing. The darkness cannot overtake your enlightenment. The storm cannot ruin your resolution. You are home.

Authority of Teaching

Matthew 7.28 And it came to pass, when Jesus had ended these sayings, the people were astonished at his doctrine:

Matthew 7.29 For he taught them as one having authority, and not as the scribes.

Jeremiah 8.7-9 Yea, the stork in the heaven knoweth her appointed times; and the turtle and the crane and the swallow observe the time of their coming; but my people know not the judgment of the LORD. How do ye say, We are wise, and the law of the LORD is with us? Lo, certainly in vain made he it; the pen of the scribes is in vain. The wise men are ashamed, they are dismayed and taken: lo, they have rejected the word of the LORD; and what wisdom is in them?

Apollonius of Tyana 1.17.1 He was not given to logic-chopping or to long discourses, and he was never heard being ironic or argumentative with his listeners. In answering he spoke as if ex cathedra, saying "I know," "I believe," "Where are you off to?" "You ought to know." His sentences were short and lapidary, his vocabulary correct and fitted to the circumstances, and his sayings had the ring of commandments issued from a throne. When some quibbler asked him why he did not engage in inquiry, he replied, "Because I inquired in my youth; now it is my duty not to inquire but to teach what I have found." And when the man asked him next, "How will a wise man converse?" he replied, "Like a lawgiver: for a lawgiver must make his own convictions into ordinances for the man." This is how he conversed in Antioch, winning the admiration of people completely without culture.

Apollonius of Tyana 1.1.2 Being conversant with the gods, [Pythagoras] had learned what makes them angry or pleased with mankind, and on this he based his teachings about nature. Others, he said, merely guessed about the divine and had contradictory views about it, whereas he had been visited by Apollo, who fully admitted his identity, and also (though they did not confess it) by Athena, the Muses, and other gods, whose shapes and names were quite unknown to humanity.

To know the unknown, actually have direct firsthand experience instead of blind faith, to channel the divine instead of quoting ancient scriptures, this Greek ideal of the perfect "lover of Wisdom" [Philo-sopher] was encapsulated in Jesus. It was his religion, his foundation, it was what he hoped to inspire the world with, what he hoped would change the world to becoming more ideal. It is from these direct insights that it was hoped that those who understood the message would take these ideals as tools for change. To build the house of personal spiritual sanity on this rock could be extended to building stronger families, stronger communities, and if the dream fire was kept alive, to construct the framework for a better world, an evolved humanity, a heaven on earth.

Synergy Results in Synchronicity

So how can we wrap up the Sermon on the Mount into one thought?

There have been many components assembled to make up Christianity's vision of the nature and purpose of Jesus. Here we have no narrative, no named disciples, no miracles, and no events. Here we have no Christology, no thoughts on the questions like "is Jesus divine" or "is Jesus the Messiah" or "how does Jesus save us" that make up later Christian writings, creeds, and conclusions of official councils. Here we don't even have the expected back-to-back parable format of instruction that make up the majority of the "red letter" words in the Gospel of Matthew. What we do have is a concise set of philosophical truths, spiritual convictions tried and true from the direct experiences of those who have wanted to live lives more sacred and connected to God than that of the surrounding so-called normal world. So what then is the message of Jesus in this famous sermon? What is the answer from the ultimate guru on the ultimate mountain top?

Synergy with other people, amplified by compassion, forgiveness, and the extension of the definition of family is the first key offered. This all for one and one for all mindset means that people can build together, take care of those in need, share the skills, shall the wealth, share the knowledge, and form a utopian cosmopolitan community that could, in theory, extend to the entire planet. What if we erased the lines that divided us from them, family from enemies, children of light from children of darkness, saved from damned? There is a lot of humanitarian hopefulness in this social gospel set on everyone letting their lights shine, everyone striving for purity and perfection, everyone building strong foundations for strong families, strong communities, and socialist safety nets for those in need. Live simply and share. Forgive and encourage. Keep it real.

Synergy with God, amplified by prayer, trust in providence, love for the good, retreat from the evil, results in a spiritual synergy that creates miracles, the synchronicity of events falling into place. This harmony is the natural state of being. It is not some alien state that we need to abandon our natural way of being to attain. It is getting back to the way it is meant to be for each of us. We have loaded onto our realities fabrics of greed and mistrust and revenge. We have filled our world with imagined lines dividing peace and war, dividing rich and poor, dividing like us and foreign. We must unlearn these human held up distractions from the religions, the politics, the cultures, the traditions, the medias, and from whatever else gets in the way of clear vision. Even the thought of "Jesus saves" can distract us from the message of Jesus here.

It has been noted that the Gospel of Matthew is divided into five parts, modeled after the five "books of Moses" in the Jewish scriptures. Where the first "book of Moses" begins is with the first "man" losing the innocent bliss of the garden where he could walk with God as a close companion. Here Jesus represents the "son of man" finding his way back into the garden, rediscovering the innocence, refinding the natural inner light, and reestablishing a strong foundation of understanding and vision. As such Jesus represents a going home path, offered in free and simple terms to any who wish to follow. The old Jesus (Joshua) brought the chosen people into their promised land. The new Jesus is having those who have ears to hear to follow him across the spiritual Jordan into the kingdom of God that lives as a light shining in each of our hearts.

Mountain Meeting

Dead Sea Scrolls Community Rule 1QS 3.24 – 4.4 Yet the God of Israel (and the Angel of His Truth) assist all the Sons of Light. It is actually He who created the spirits of light and darkness, making them the cornerstone of every deed, their impulses the premise of every action. God's love for one spirit lasts forever. He will be pleased with its actions for always. The counsel of the other, however, He abhors, hating its every impulse for all time. Upon earth their operations are these: one enlightens a man's mind, making straight before him the paths of true righteousness and causing his heart to fear the laws of God. This spirit engenders humility, patience, abundant compassion, perpetual goodness, insight, understanding, and powerful wisdom resonating to each of God's deeds, sustained by His constant faithfulness.

I think there has been this idea that the dark forces have held human culture in sway to where you have to get beyond the boundaries of civilization to find the light forces. The Dead Sea Scrolls community went to the wilderness to re-find God. The idea of getting away from it all to re-connect has been attempted many times, Amish-like, in the history of humanity. The idea of climbing that sacred mountain to find that which eludes the masses is an archetype that seems timeless and across cultures.

The problem with the Law of Moses was that it had become so filtered through centuries of tradition. Was what the scribes claimed was the Law really the Message of God as given to Moses on that mountain centuries before? A Direct Connect was needed to climb back up the mountain and give a New Testament from God to his people. The "Sons of Light" people of the Dead Sea Scrolls envisioned "The Messenger of Truth" directly connecting to God and personally teaching through the authority of this direct connection. That was the vision for the Sermon on the Mountain. Jesus was that Messenger of Truth, that new Joshua.

Mount Athos

Apollonius of Tyana 2.5.3 "But though I have climbed this mountain that is the highest of all, I shall come down it none the wiser." "Nor did they," said Apollonius. "Such vantage points show the heaven more brilliant, the stars bigger, and the sun rising during the night, but such things are evident to shepherds and goatherd too. But how the Deity cares about the human race, and how it loves to receives worship from it, what virtue is and justice and chastity, all this Athos will not reveal to those who climb it, nor will the famous Olympus so admired by the poets, unless the soul discerns them. If it is pure and unblemished when it apprehends them, in my opinion it soars much higher than the Caucasus here."

Mount Olympus

Homer: Odyssey 3.9.6 When she had said this Minerva went away to Olympus, which they say is the everlasting home of the gods. Here no wind beats roughly, and neither rain nor snow can fall; but it abides in everlasting sunshine and in a great peacefulness of light, wherein the blessed gods are illumined for ever and ever. This was the place to which the goddess went when she had given instructions to the girl.

Minerva in the Odyssey serves as a companion "Holy Spirit" intercessor and synchronizer for Ulysses / Odysseus. The ascension into Olympus and the idea of the "heaven" of Olympus reminds us of Jesus ascending into heaven. As Minerva went to Olympus to be with her father Jove, so Jesus went to heaven to be with his Father God. A Greek audience in the time at which the gospels were first being presented would not have failed to see the resonance here. In the Sermon on the Mount, we are carried up onto the sacred mountain to be taught from this lofty perspective directly. Enough with the division of sacred priests who own and control the message for the ignorant flock. Everyone who climbs the mountain and is taught the message walks back down as an initiated priest. We are all insiders now. No more secrets, for they are shouted from the rooftops. No more being kept in the dark, for we are each taught how to light our own way.

Mount Sinai

Exodus 19.10-11 And the LORD said unto Moses, Go unto the people, and sanctify them to day and to morrow, and let them wash their clothes, and be ready against the third day: for the third day the LORD will come down in the sight of all the people upon mount Sinai.

Exodus 19.15-20 And he said unto the people, Be ready against the third day: come not at your wives. And it came to pass on the third day in the morning, that there were thunders and lightnings, and a thick cloud upon the mount, and the voice of the trumpet exceeding loud; so that all the people that was in the camp trembled. And Moses brought forth the people out of the camp to meet with God; and they stood at the nether part of the mount. And mount Sinai was altogether on a smoke, because the LORD descended upon it in fire: and the smoke thereof ascended as the smoke of a furnace, and the whole mount quaked greatly. And when the voice of the trumpet sounded long, and waxed louder and louder, Moses spake, and God answered him by a voice. And the LORD came down upon mount Sinai, on the top of the mount: and the LORD called Moses up to the top of the mount; and Moses went up.

In the Sermon on the Mount, we are all, as readers, as Moses on the mountain hearing the "word" of the Lord. Jesus represents God's "word", and just as God gave instructions to Moses, so Jesus instructs his disciples. We have access to the message now, not just second hand hearsay. We don't have to trust in ancient texts, translated, interpreted, which could not be equal to actually being Moses standing by his burning bush. The Sermon on the Mount was in the language of the early Christians, fresh and alive. It had no ancient history, no sacred scrolls, and no special place in a temple. It plugged in the common spiritual seeker directly. We can descend the mountain with our own gnosis, our own direct encounter, our own collected wisdom.

Mount Gerizim

John 4.20-21 Our fathers worshipped in this mountain; and ye say, that in Jerusalem is the place where men ought to worship. Jesus saith unto her, Woman, believe me, the hour cometh, when ye shall neither in this mountain, nor yet at Jerusalem, worship the Father.

Mount Gerizim was sacred to the Samaritans in the same way that the Temple in Jerusalem was sacred to the Jews. It was the sacred site that Abraham had offered Isaac in sacrifice to God (Genesis 22.2). While the Temple in Jerusalem was destroyed in 70 and Jews forbidden to enter the city after the defeat of Simon ben Kosiba in 135, the Temple of Gerizim was rebuilt and remained active. Mount Gerizim was the Mount of Blessing that Joshua / Jesus son of Nun had deemed as the first holy place in Israel after having crossed the Jordan River. The Samaritan position (Samaritan Chronicle Adler) was that the "sons of Eli" had abandoned Mount Gerizim and had moved (1 Samuel 1.3) and desecrated (1 Samuel 2.12) the faith. The Eli Temple at Shiloh was a copy of the Temple at Mount Gerizim. This sets up the scene for the Sermon on the Mount. Here we have the voice of "Joshua / Jesus" revived, standing against the perversions and corruptions of the true faith and reviving the ancient purity of heart that is older and stronger than the Jerusalem set of rules and regulations.

Deuteronomy 11.29 And it shall come to pass, when the LORD thy God hath brought thee in unto the land whither thou goest to possess it, that thou shalt put the blessing upon mount Gerizim, and the curse upon mount Ebal.

Deuteronomy 27.12 These shall stand upon mount Gerizim to bless the people, when ye are come over Jordan; Simeon, and Levi, and Judah, and Issachar, and Joseph, and Benjamin:

Judges 9.7 And when they told it to Jotham, he went and stood in the top of mount Gerizim, and lifted up his voice, and cried, and said unto them, Hearken unto me, ye men of Shechem, that God may hearken unto you.

It is interesting that the most famous sermon of Jesus is this "Sermon on the Mount" and not a "Sermon in the Jerusalem Temple." The Jesus incident in the temple had him cracking a whip and turning over tables, not delivering the word of God to the people there.

Mount of Olives

Josephus: The Wars of the Jews 2.13.5 But there was an Egyptian false prophet that did the Jews more mischief than the former; for he was a cheat, and pretended to be a prophet also, and got together thirty thousand men that were deluded by him; these he led round about from the wilderness to the mount which was called the Mount of Olives, and was ready to break into Jerusalem by force from that place; and if he could but once conquer the Roman garrison and the people, he intended to domineer over them by the assistance of those guards of his that were to break into the city with him.

Josephus: The Antiquities of the Jews 20.9.6 Moreover, there came out of Egypt about this time to Jerusalem, one that said he was a prophet, and advised the multitude of the common people to go along with him to the Mount of Olives, as it was called, which lay over against the city, and at the distance of five furlongs. He said farther, that he would show them from hence, how, at his command, the walls of Jerusalem would fall down; and he promised that he would procure them an entrance into the city through those walls, when they were fallen down.

Jesus with the Sermon on the Mount is the antithesis of the Egyptian Messianic pretender on the Mount of Olives. The message of Jesus was one of peace and love for the enemy. The Egyptian promised his followers that God would be on their side and the Jerusalem walls would crumble as God gave them control of the city. This reminds us of the fall of Jericho's wall when the prophet Joshua / Jesus arrived there. In the Greek LXX, the prophet Joshua is Iesous, the same as the Greek spelling of Jesus. The two being the same must have struck early Greek speaking Christians looking for references to their Jesus in the Jewish scriptures speaking of this prophet Jesus from ancient times. Either the new Jesus had to be an echo of the power and purpose of the old Jesus, or the new Jesus had to be the antithesis of the old Jesus.

Joshua 6.2 And the LORD said unto Joshua, See, I have given into thine hand Jericho, and the king thereof, and the mighty men of valour.

Joshua 6.20 So the people shouted when the priests blew with the trumpets: and it came to pass, when the people heard the sound of the trumpet, and the people shouted with a great shout, that the wall fell down flat, so that the people went up into the city, every man straight before him, and they took the city.

This "out of Egypt" self-proclaimed prophet who could summon the power to knock down walls and lead the people to take a city is unnamed by Josephus, but the prophet Joshua / Jesus definitely comes to mind. I can imagine there being ideas at the time that if there was a new prophet Joshua who could come out of obscurity in Egypt and lead the chosen people to the promised kingdom, past rivers and walls, this would have been wrapped up with the MaSHiYaCH (Messiah) concept. It is interesting that the Joshua / Jesus MaSHiYaCH / Christ Egyptian savior prophet reference by Josephus stood on his mountain giving his sermon to his followers. If you read on in the story told by Josephus, four hundred were killed, two hundred were taken prisoner, and this Joshua / Jesus MaSHiYaCH / Christ Egyptian savior prophet ran away and was never heard from again. Contrast this to the Joshua / Jesus of the Sermon on the Mount. The title Christ does not appear in Matthew chapters 5 through 7. The Jesus of this sermon does not claim that title. His message of peace and love is the exact opposite of the message expected for the militant Christ to come on the clouds of war horses of divine fury. His promised kingdom was not of this world, and the walls he envisioned as falling down were the ones dividing people. He was not rallying the people to take up the zeal of violence, as the Joshua / Jesus Jewish prophet had accomplished. He was supporting a peaceful and harmonious cooperative living with the foreign forces. He promoted ideas changing the landscape of Jewish life and thought. He taught more like a Buddha than a Jewish prophet. Could he have imagined the later bloody crusades to be fought in his name? The inquisitions and witch hunts? The conquistadors and manifest destiny?

Josephus was an educated Jew that sympathized with the Romans and documented the waves of violent revolutionary sects among his own people. If Josephus could have invented a counter to his noted wave of terrorist thugs, a Jewish "true prophet" that stood up for the best virtues of Judaism without the sharp edges of xenophobia and violence, I could imagine him proposing the gentle spoken Jesus with the messages of the Sermon on the Mount.

To Every People

YUNUS 10.47 To every people (was sent) a messenger: when their messenger comes (before them), the matter will be judged between them with justice, and they will not be wronged.

To every people is an interesting term. That spans all nations of people, all ethnic groups, and all religious traditions. That spans all ages before Muhammad's time. That also spans all ages AFTER Muhammad's time. What do you suppose the Word would look like sent as a Message from the Oneness of God to your people, your nation, your generation, your way of thinking and talking about things? To every people includes you.

AL NAHL 16.36 For We assuredly sent amongst every People a messenger, (with the Command), "Serve Allah, and eschew Evil": of the People were some whom Allah guided, and some on whom error became inevitably (established). So travel through the earth, and see what was the end of those who denied (the Truth).

AL NAHL 16.84 One Day We shall raise from all Peoples a Witness: then will no excuse be accepted from Unbelievers, nor will they receive any favours.

This is even presented in FUTURE TENSE here. The day will come when there will be representatives of, witnesses of, prophets of, experiences of contact with, comprehenders of part of the pattern of the Oneness of God. Someone will be getting it anywhere and at any time you happen to be. No matter what town you are in and what the current date is on the calendar, someone around you gets it. Someone around everyone gets it. So many people will Witness to getting it that no one could possibly be left that hasn't heard about the story of someone getting it. What it is to get is what Muhammad got, what Jesus got, what we all need to get. Then what there is to do is to become a Witness to this Oneness of God to those around us in our own sphere of influence.

AL RA'D 13.38 We did send messengers before thee, and appointed for them wives and children: and it was never the part of a messenger to bring a sign except as Allah permitted (or commanded). For each period is a Book (revealed).

As we have seen in this study, some of the thoughts presented in these books still apply to our day and situations.

AL BAQARAH 2.285 The Messenger believeth in what hath been revealed to him from his Lord, as do the men of faith. Each one (of them) believeth in Allah, His angels, His books, and His messengers. "We make no distinction (they say) between one and another of His messengers." And they say: "We hear, and we obey: (We seek) Thy forgiveness, our Lord, and to Thee is the end of all journeys."

AL MA'IDAH 5.54 O ye who believe! if any from among you turn back from his Faith, soon will Allah produce a people whom He will love as they will love Him – lowly with the believers, mighty against the rejecters, fighting in the way of Allah, and never afraid of the reproaches of such as find fault. That is the grace of Allah, which He will bestow on whom He pleaseth. And Allah encompasseth all, and He knoweth all things.

Matthew 3.8-9 Bring forth therefore fruits meet for repentance: and think not to say within yourselves, We have Abraham to our father; for I say unto you, that God is able of these stones to raise up children unto Abraham.

FATIR 35.31 That which We have revealed to thee of the Book is the Truth – confirming what was (revealed) before it: for Allah is assuredly – with respect to His Servants – well acquainted and Fully Observant.

Hardly anything that is completely new is worthwhile. Most every great invention, every quantum leap inducing insight, rests on the foundation of previous revelations. The honest ones admit they are derivative of previously stated ideas. Christians, for the most part, are not familiar with the non-Christian texts presented in this book, or even the Gnostic and Apocryphal Christian references. As such, their Jesus speaks in a vacuum of uniqueness in their Bible-only mindset. What we have observed in this study is the resonance of thought throughout a wide spectrum of spiritual traditions, cultures, and ages. As such, Jesus is not alien to humanity, not speaking a new message from beyond our cosmos. Jesus, rather, reflects back to us the best ideas we have considered with positive feedback and encouragement, and weaves them into a fabric, a Dharma, a Gospel. This fabric becomes a foundation constructed for those who want to build upon these ideals, a solution to our quest for immortality and meaning, gnosis of who we truly are and how we connect to one another and to God.

Matthew 13.51-52 Jesus saith unto them, Have ye understood all these things? They say unto him, Yea, Lord. Then said he unto them, Therefore every scribe which is instructed unto the kingdom of heaven is like unto a man that is an householder, which bringeth forth out of his treasure things new and old.

Mark

This entire block of sayings is represented in Mark as only five isolated verses. I think Mark knew the Sermon on the Mount, but it was a separate and beloved text that complimented the gospel story he had to tell. The values are woven in, but not so many quotes are shared, as if Mark was for outsiders and the Sermon on the Mount and other teachings were for initiates. The two collections were woven together in Matthew.

Mark 9.49 For every one shall be salted with fire, and every sacrifice shall be salted with salt.

"Salted with fire" is a Mark-only concept. The Aramaic word for "salted" also means "scattered", the symbolism being the parts to be eliminated in the refining process are popping away left and right in the heat of the purification process.

Mark 9.50 Salt is good: but if the salt have lost his saltness, wherewith will ye season it? Have salt in yourselves, and have peace one with another.

What is this Salt? This Inner Salt leads to peace one with another. It is something that if you lose it, how could you ever get it back? In occult practices, pouring a circle of salt on the ground protects from evil spirits. It is establishing a very localized holy site, dedicated to being pure and undefiled. Symbolically salt is spirituality, religion itself, but what happens when religion becomes the problem instead of the protection from the problems?

Mark 4.21 And he said unto them, Is a candle brought to be put under a bushel, or under a bed? And not to be set on a candlestick?

What is this Candle? What is the meaning of putting this Candle on a candlestick as compared with under a bushel or under a bed? Is Candle like Salt? Does it represent an Inner Light? A social gospel? Sharing is the key here, sharing what little light you may have acquired. What if a thousand people shared their candle lights? It could illuminate the dark night in an amazing way.

Mark 11.25 And when ye stand praying, forgive, if ye have ought against any: that your Father also which is in heaven may forgive you your trespasses.

Forgiveness requires being forgiving. God will cut you some slack for getting things wrong if you cut some slack to those around you when they get things wrong. Change is subjective, very personal. It is all in your mind. Change yourself and you become changed.

Mark 4.24 And he said unto them, Take heed what ye hear: with what measure ye mete, it shall be measured to you: and unto you that hear shall more be given.

The more of the message you put into practice, the more of the message you will then come to understand. Like the way you can learn more from a subject in school after studying it for a few years as compared to when you first signed up, spiritual truths become clearer the more you collect of them.

Mark 1.22 And they were astonished at his doctrine: for he taught them as one that had authority, and not as the scribes.

The scribes merely repeat back what they have memorized. Jesus was presenting concepts that had to be directly lived out. His authority was the practicality of spiritual development when activated by direct experience.

Luke

Mark 4:34 But without a parable spake he not unto them: and when they were alone, he expounded all things to his disciples.

Mark purposefully excluded the secret inner teachings, such as that of the Sermon on the Mount, but Luke wanted to incorporate them, give the reader a sense of being there, as one of the disciples listening to the Master.

As is evident by this collection, once the overtly Jewish material was cut out of the Sermon on the Mount, the remainder does not stand as a coherent whole, thus Luke dispersed the material throughout his gospel.

[Matthew 5.16-17] To make Jesus comply with the Epistles, the reference to good works and praise for the law was omitted.

[Matthew 5.19-20] To make Jesus comply with the Epistles, the reference to not breaking commandments and righteousness contrasted with the scribes was omitted.

[Matthew 5.33-37] The rules for swearing to oaths were omitted as it applied to Jewish legalism.

[Matthew 5.41] Omitted because this is specifically a practice of Roman soldiers forcing civilians to assist in their carrying supplies.

[Matthew 5.45] What does this mean in terms of spirituality? This is dogmatically vague, thus omitted.

[Matthew 6.1-3] Perhaps it was the idea of being rewarded in heaven for actually having done something good that got this section omitted in the quest for making Jesus comply with the justification by faith doctrine of the Epistles.

[Matthew 6.14-15] This concept would be opposed to justification by faith.

[Matthew 6.16-18] Fasting omitted.

[Matthew 7.6] This could be seen as xenophobic slurs at non-Jews, which would not be appropriate for a Roman or Greek audience.

The idea that there was a separate "Q" document that both Matthew and Luke used as a "source" in different ways is being challenged here. I propose that Luke knew of the Sermon on the Mount as a complete thought, whether separate from or included in the Gospel of Matthew, and selectively used what material would suit a gospel designed for a non-Jewish audience. Here is the Sermon on the Mount as adopted by Luke. Notice how it could be a sermon given by a pagan philosopher. It is a true cosmopolitan message to transcend Judaism, and to even transcend its age and world, to be relevant to this very day and time. That was obviously the plan.

Luke 4.32 And they were astonished at his doctrine: for his word was with power.

Luke 6.20 And he lifted up his eyes on his disciples, and said, Blessed be ye poor: for yours is the kingdom of God.

Luke 6.21 Blessed are ye that hunger now: for ye shall be filled. Blessed are ye that weep now: for ye shall laugh.

Luke 6.22 Blessed are ye, when men shall hate you, and when they shall separate you from their company, and shall reproach you, and cast out your name as evil, for the Son of man's sake.

Luke 6.23 Rejoice ye in that day, and leap for joy: for, behold, your reward is great in heaven: for in the like manner did their fathers unto the prophets.

Luke 6.27 But I say unto you which hear, Love your enemies, do good to them which hate you,

Luke 6.28 Bless them that curse you, and pray for them which despitefully use you.

Luke 6.29 And unto him that smiteth thee on the one cheek offer also the other; and him that taketh away thy cloak forbid not to take thy coat also.

Luke 6.30 Give to every man that asketh of thee; and of him that taketh away thy goods ask them not again.

Luke 6.31 And as ye would that men should do to you, do ye also to them likewise.

146

Luke 6.32 For if ye love them which love you, what thank have ye? For sinners also love those that love them.

Luke 6.33 And if ye do good to them which do good to you, what thank have ye? For sinners also do even the same.

Luke seems to use part of the sentiment of Matthew 5:45 here. He is trying to make the idea practical, one of lending money. Luke speaks of lending money and then omits the following alms section. Alms are mentioned in Luke 12:33.

Luke 6.34 And if ye lend to them of whom ye hope to receive, what thank have ye? For sinners also lend to sinners, to receive as much again.

Luke 6.35 But love ye your enemies, and do good, and lend, hoping for nothing again; and your reward shall be great, and ye shall be the children of the Highest: for he is kind unto the unthankful and to the evil.

This is an interesting verse. Within traditional Judaism, God is merciful to those who are grateful and strive to be good people. Who is this "Highest" Father God that is kind to the unthankful and evil of the world? Marcion concluded that this "Highest" was alien to the God described by Jewish tradition.

Luke 6.36 Be ye therefore merciful, as your Father also is merciful.

Be "perfect" is replaced with be "merciful" – this shifts the focus from obeying every last dictate of the Law to striving to become a living channel for merciful loving kindness to flow. The idea of perfection comes with connotations that the goal may be impossible. But we can all advance in being merciful, having empathy, having sympathy, sharing compassion.

Luke 6.37 Judge not, and ye shall not be judged: condemn not, and ye shall not be condemned: forgive, and ye shall be forgiven:

Luke 6.38 Give, and it shall be given unto you; good measure, pressed down, and shaken together, and running over, shall men give into your bosom. For with the same measure that ye mete withal it shall be measured to you again.

Luke 6.41 And why beholdest thou the mote that is in thy brother's eye, but perceivest not the beam that is in thine own eye?

Luke 6.42 Either how canst thou say to thy brother, Brother, let me pull out the mote that is in thine eye, when thou thyself beholdest not the beam that is in thine own eye? Thou hypocrite, cast out first the beam out of thine own eye, and then shalt thou see clearly to pull out the mote that is in thy brother's eye.

Luke 6.43 For a good tree bringeth not forth corrupt fruit; neither doth a corrupt tree bring forth good fruit.

Luke 6.44 For every tree is known by his own fruit. For of thorns men do not gather figs, nor of a bramble bush gather they grapes.

Luke 6.46 And why call ye me, Lord, Lord, and do not the things which I say?

This is an interesting comment, implying that Christianity formed that defines Jesus as "Lord" and yet doesn't center upon his teachings. The "doeth the will of my Father" from Matthew 7.21 is here replaced with the doing of what Jesus said.

Luke 6.47 Whosoever cometh to me, and heareth my sayings, and doeth them, I will shew you to whom he is like:

Luke 6.48 He is like a man which built an house, and digged deep, and laid the foundation on a rock: and when the flood arose, the stream beat vehemently upon that house, and could not shake it: for it was founded upon a rock.

Luke 6.49 But he that heareth, and doeth not, is like a man that without a foundation built an house upon the earth; against which the stream did beat vehemently, and immediately it fell; and the ruin of that house was great.

Luke 8.16 No man, when he hath lighted a candle, covereth it with a vessel, or putteth it under a bed; but setteth it on a candlestick, that they which enter in may see the light.

Such an important thought, it was used twice in Luke (8.16 and 11.33).

Luke 11.1 And it came to pass, that, as he was praying in a certain place, when he ceased, one of his disciples said unto him, Lord, teach us to pray, as John also taught his disciples.

Luke 11.2 And he said unto them, When ye pray, say, Our Father which art in heaven, Hallowed be thy name. Thy kingdom come. Thy will be done, as in heaven, so in earth.

Notice the great variation in this verse from the King James to the New International version: He said to them, "When you pray, say: '"Father, hallowed by your name, your kingdom come.

Luke 11.3 Give us day by day our daily bread.

Luke 11.4 And forgive us our sins; for we also forgive every one that is indebted to us. And lead us not into temptation; but deliver us from evil.

Luke 11.9 And I say unto you, Ask, and it shall be given you; seek, and ye shall find; knock, and it shall be opened unto you.

Luke 11.10 For every one that asketh receiveth; and he that seeketh findeth; and to him that knocketh it shall be opened.

Luke 11.11 If a son shall ask bread of any of you that is a father, will he give him a stone? Or if he ask a fish, will he for a fish give him a serpent?

Luke 11.12 Or if he shall ask an egg, will he offer him a scorpion?

Luke 11.13 If ye then, being evil, know how to give good gifts unto your children: how much more shall your heavenly Father give the Holy Spirit to them that ask him?

The "good things" of Matthew 7.11 is changed to "Holy Spirit" in Luke 11.13. Some versions read "good Spirit", some read "Holy Spirit from heaven".

Luke 11.33 No man, when he hath lighted a candle, putteth it in a secret place, neither under a bushel, but on a candlestick, that they which come in may see the light.

Some versions read "in the cellar" instead of "under a bushel".

Luke 11.34 The light of the body is the eye: therefore when thine eye is single, thy whole body also is full of light; but when thine eye is evil, thy body also is full of darkness.

Luke 11.35 Take heed therefore that the light which is in thee be not darkness.

Luke 12.22 And he said unto his disciples, Therefore I say unto you, Take no thought for your life, what ye shall eat; neither for the body, what ye shall put on.

Luke 12.23 The life is more than meat, and the body is more than raiment.

Luke 12.24 Consider the ravens: for they neither sow nor reap; which neither have storehouse nor barn; and God feedeth them: how much more are ye better than the fowls?

Luke 12.25 And which of you with taking thought can add to his stature one cubit?

Luke 12.27 Consider the lilies how they grow: they toil not, they spin not; and yet I say unto you, that Solomon in all his glory was not arrayed like one of these.

Some versions add "nor weave" after "spin not".

Luke 12.28 If then God so clothe the grass, which is today in the field, and tomorrow is cast into the oven; how much more will he clothe you, O ye of little faith?

Luke 12.29 And seek not ye what ye shall eat, or what ye shall drink, neither be ye of doubtful mind.

Luke 12.30 For all these things do the nations of the world seek after: and your Father knoweth that ye have need of these things.

Luke 12.31 But rather seek ye the kingdom of God; and all these things shall be added unto you.

Some versions have "His kingdom" in place of "kingdom of God".

Luke 12.32 Fear not, little flock; for it is your Father's good pleasure to give you the kingdom.

Luke 12.33 Sell that ye have, and give alms; provide yourselves bags which wax not old, a treasure in the heavens that faileth not, where no thief approacheth, neither moth corrupteth.

Luke 12.34 For where your treasure is, there will your heart be also.

Luke 12.57 Yea, and why even of yourselves judge ye not what is right?

Luke 12.58 When thou goest with thine adversary to the magistrate, as thou art in the way, give diligence that thou mayest be delivered from him; lest he hale thee to the judge, and the judge deliver thee to the officer, and the officer cast thee into prison.

Luke 12.59 I tell thee, thou shalt not depart thence, till thou hast paid the very last mite.

Luke 13.22 And he went through the cities and villages, teaching, and journeying toward Jerusalem.

Luke 13.23 Then said one unto him, Lord, are there few that be saved? And he said unto them,

Luke 13.24 Strive to enter in at the strait gate: for many, I say unto you, will seek to enter in, and shall not be able.

In Luke's expansion here, we see Jesus telling the Jews that they were unknown to the real God of Abraham, that their pretense of religion had become so perverted that they no longer had a connection. Then he goes on to explain (Luke 13.28) that other people, gentiles, from around the world will connect to this real God of Abraham and discover what the Jews had lost focus of. The focus upon Abraham is interesting in that this is the identification of Islam as having rediscovered and restored the original connection to God that was thought to have had become perverted and distorted in both Jewish and Christian traditions.

Luke 13.25 When once the master of the house is risen up, and hath shut to the door, and ye begin to stand without, and to knock at the door, saying, Lord, Lord, open unto us; and he shall answer and say unto you, I know you not whence ye are:

Luke 13.26 Then shall ye begin to say, We have eaten and drunk in thy presence, and thou hast taught in our streets.

Luke 13.27 But he shall say, I tell you, I know you not whence ye are; depart from me, all ye workers of iniquity.

Luke 14.34 Salt is good: but if the salt have lost his savour, wherewith shall it be seasoned?

Luke 14.35 It is neither fit for the land, nor yet for the dunghill; but men cast it out. He that hath ears to hear, let him hear.

How could you take salt, which is supposed to purify and protect against evil, and corrupt it? Once corrupted, salt (religion, spiritual tradition) couldn't have any effect in making a magic circle on the land, it couldn't do shit, it is useless trash. Don't corrupt your salt. It is there to help you preserve your spiritual space in an unspiritual world. If you don't protect its purity, how will you ever get it back?

Luke 16.13 No servant can serve two masters: for either he will hate the one, and love the other; or else he will hold to the one, and despise the other. Ye cannot serve God and mammon.

The Pharisee Reaction to the derision of mammon by Jesus is unique to Luke.

Luke 16.14 And the Pharisees also, who were covetous, heard all these things: and they derided him.

Luke 16.15 And he said unto them, Ye are they which justify yourselves before men; but God knoweth your hearts: for that which is highly esteemed among men is abomination in the sight of God.

Luke 16.16 The law and the prophets were until John: since that time the kingdom of God is preached, and every man presseth into it.

Luke 16.17 And it is easier for heaven and earth to pass, than one tittle of the law to fail.

In light of Luke 16.16, the line had been drawn between the Old Testament of Law and Prophets and the New Testament of directly pressing into the kingdom of God. In Marcion's version of Luke, it wasn't that one part of the old law couldn't fail, it was rather that one part of the new gospel message "law" of Jesus couldn't fail.

Luke 16.18 Whosoever putteth away his wife, and marrieth another, committeth adultery: and whosoever marrieth her that is put away from her husband committeth adultery.

Interesting that this one thought was preserved while so many others were edited out. It stands as the only example of unfailing law. The following verse in Luke begins a new parable.

Before you can dream to love your neighbor or even your enemy, love must begin at home. The one that you took in to be your spouse, your mate, your partner in raising your children, should be the closest person to you on the planet. In a world of fractured values, to devote a life to the idea of love brings family values to the focal point. Perhaps this is the true cornerstone of a life devoted to love. Respect love beyond all obstacles that stand in its way.

The Power of the Good

Shepherd of Hermas Mandate 8 1.8-10 "Sir," say I, "show me the power of the good also, that I may walk in them and serve them, that doing them it may be possible for me to be saved." "Hear," saith he, "the works of the good likewise, which thou must do, and towards which thou must exercise no self-restraint. First of all, there is faith, fear of the Lord, love, concord, words of righteousness, truth, patience; nothing is better than these in the life of men. If a man keep these, and exercise not self-restraint from them, he becomes blessed in his life. Hear now what follow upon these; to minister to widows, to visit the orphans and the needy, to ransom the servants of God from their afflictions, to be hospitable (for in hospitality benevolence from time to time has a place), to resist no man, to be tranquil, to show yourself more submissive than all men, to reverence the aged, to practice righteousness, to observe brotherly feeling, to endure injury, to be long-suffering, to bear no grudge, to exhort those who are sick at soul, not to cast away those that have stumbled from the faith, but to convert them and to put courage into them, to reprove sinners, not to oppress debtors and indigent persons, and whatsoever actions are like these.

Snapshot into early Christianity is presented here. Early Christians would read the Sermon on the Mount in the context of other early Christian texts. Today, most of these texts are virtually unknown to the majority of Christians.

I encourage all readers, Christian and non-Christian alike, to explore in more depth the texts that have small excerpt quotes included in this book. They each have much more to offer in general as well as in specific resonance with the teachings and life of Jesus, which will be explored in subsequent volumes in this series. I know there are gems in each of these that can inspire and challenge, paradigm shift and amaze, align and enlighten.

Bottom Line: Agape

1 John 4.7 Beloved, let us love one another: for love is of God; and every one that loveth is born of God, and knoweth God.

In the Greek original, the word for love is agape. This form of love is a feeling of connection, of family, as a brotherly love for a close relative, affection, a sense of wanting things to go right for those in your inner circle of friends.

Matthew 19.19 Honour thy father and thy mother: and, Thou shalt love thy neighbour as thyself.

Imagine a world where we take the family values we got from our parents and extended these manners and courtesies to the people we encounter in our lives as we venture out into the world outside of the walls of our childhood home.

Luke 11.11-13 If a son shall ask bread of any of you that is a father, will he give him a stone? or if he ask a fish, will he for a fish give him a serpent? Or if he shall ask an egg, will he offer him a scorpion? If ye then, being evil, know how to give good gifts unto your children: how much more shall your heavenly Father give the Holy Spirit to them that ask him?

Maybe your parents weren't perfect, but they did manage to feed you, they considered you to be family, that you belonged to them, that they were responsible for you. There is this lasting bond. You can return to visit them and it feels like home. It is this sense of family values that we have to hold and copy into other parts of our lives.

Mark 10.6-9 But from the beginning of the creation God made them male and female. For this cause shall a man leave his father and mother, and cleave to his wife; And they twain shall be one flesh: so then they are no more twain, but one flesh. What therefore God hath joined together, let not man put asunder.

When you decide to get married to another person, this is adopting them into your own personal sense of family. You take on the same name, live in the same house, and raise the same children. This person, who you used to not know, is now related to you. Jesus taught that this added relationship should be as unbreakable to you as the relationship you have with your parents and with your children. This sense of sacred family values is core to the message of Jesus.

Mark 12.30-31 And thou shalt love the Lord thy God with all thy heart, and with all thy soul, and with all thy mind, and with all thy strength: this is the first commandment. And the second is like, namely this, Thou shalt love thy neighbour as thyself. There is none other commandment greater than these.

You have your immediate family, your parents, your children, your spouse. Beyond the definitions of family relationships, there are people in the world out there, next door, down the street, in the stores, on the roads, at work, in restaurants. What if you thought of all of them as part of an extended family?

Matthew 5.44-45 But I say unto you, Love your enemies, bless them that curse you, do good to them that hate you, and pray for them which despitefully use you, and persecute you; That ye may be the children of your Father which is in heaven: for he maketh his sun to rise on the evil and on the good, and sendeth rain on the just and on the unjust.

Beyond the people who are similar to you and share the same traditions and histories, there are foreigners with different values, different religions, and different lifestyles. There are people with different politics, different passions, different conclusions, and different agendas. What if you thought of all of them as part of an extended global family?

John 13.35 By this shall all men know that ye are my disciples, if ye have love one to another.

The word know in this verse is a form of the word gnosis, which means to have knowledge that is direct and personal, that you recognize, that is familiar to you. The discernable family trait of someone who understands the message of Jesus is that of an all-embracing agape.

By such an expansion of the definition of family and the accompanying flowing of the compassion, empathy, and even charity that comes with taking care of your own, those who live out this gnosis can and will change the world around them for the better. What if entire communities followed this message? Networks of communities? International organizations of people with this mindset? Love could change the world. The dream is worth trying.

Threads

Buddhist texts are called sutras or suttas, meaning threads, thoughts to be woven into the whole of a fabricated reality, a Dharma fabric, an outlook on life, a vision of how things be, an intention of how to live.

Likewise, each chapter of the Qur'an is called a surah, a thread.

The Gospel of Matthew is made up of distinct parts, one of which is a whole thought, a thread, known as the Sermon on the Mount. The other parts include the base copying of the Gospel of Mark with its journey to Jerusalem and Passion story, a Christmas story, and a collection of parables and teachings.

It is typical that quotes from spiritual texts are only from one religious tradition, but here we have a collection compiled from various cultures and ages. They are typically not seen together.

Another concept from the Qur'an is that collections of surah's, of threads, make up gems, siparah. Then the collection of siparah gems can be taken to present the whole picture, the complete understanding.

Extend this thought to the larger, cosmopolitan, collection, and take on the task of weaving the threads, collecting the gems, and observing the created fabric of Truth that transcends cultures and ages. We have a Jesus preaching, not a fundamentalist message that sees itself as the only right way and every other religion as evil, but a message that is resonated in word-encapsulated-thoughts from cultures and ages far beyond the scope of a first century CE Jerusalem.

Collections

Dead Sea Scrolls, Wise Abegg Cook version, a Jewish library collection of treasured spiritual texts preserved and hidden during the wars with the Romans in the first century CE.

DN is Digha Nikaya, early Buddhist, Maurice Walse version, The Long Discourses of the Buddha.

KJV is King James Version Bible, Christian, a royal British project in 1607. It included the Old Testament (Jewish accepted scriptures), the New Testament (Catholic Christian accepted scriptures), and the Apocrypha (Catholic Christian accepted Jewish texts that are not acknowledged as scripture by Jews, but which were known by and influenced the formation of Christianity). There is a Shakespeare play quality to the way thoughts are expressed in words, and in the way that words often end in an extra "est" or "eth". While there are more modern translations, the reason I selected KJV is for its timeless beauty and majesty. As a young Baptist, this was the version first handed to me, and the version from which I first read the Sermon on the Mount.

MN is Majjhima Nikaya, early Buddhist, Bhikkhu Nanamoli and Bhikkhu Bodhi version, The Middle Length Discourses of the Buddha.

NHL is Nag Hammadi Library, a collection of sacred early Christian Gnostic texts, preserved from the programmatic destruction of ancient texts by Catholic Christianity by being hidden away by monks who saw the value in preserving them for future generations to discover.

Qur'an (Koran) is the central sacred text of Islam, Abdullah Yusuf Ali version, a scholar from India whose translation is the most widely known and used in English.

SN is Samyutta Nikaya, early Buddhist, Bhikkhu Bodhi version, The Connected Discourses of the Buddha.

Texts

1 Chronicles: KJV, Old Testament, 1 copy found among Dead Sea Scrolls

1 Corinthians: KJV, New Testament

1 Enoch, E. Isaac version, 20 copies found among Dead Sea Scrolls, Ethiopic Apocalypse of Enoch, adopted by Christians, Chapters 37-71 added second century CE

1 John: KJV, New Testament

1 Kings: KJV, Old Testament, 3 copies found among Dead Sea Scrolls

1 Peter: KJV, New Testament

1 Samuel: KJV, Old Testament, 4 copies found among Dead Sea Scrolls

1 Timothy: KJV, New Testament

2 Chronicles, KJV, Old Testament, 1 copy found among Dead Sea Scrolls

2 Esdras, KJV, Jewish text adopted and expanded by Christians, also known as: 3 Esdras in Russian Bible, 4 Esdras in Latin Vulgate, Great Bible, and Douay Bible

2 Kings, KJV, Old Testament, 3 copies found among Dead Sea Scrolls

Akankheyya Sutta, MN 6, If a Bhikkhu should wish

AL 'ANKABUT: Qur'an surah 29, The Spider

AL 'IMRAN: Qur'an surah 3, The Family of Imran

AL A'LA: Qur'an surah 87, The Most High

AL A'RAF: Qur'an surah 7, The Heights

AL AHQAF: Qur'an surah 46, Winding Sand-tracts

AL AN'AM: Qur'an surah 6, The Cattle

AL ANBIYA: Qur'an surah 21, The Prophets

AL ANFAL: Qur'an surah 8, The Spoils of War

AL BALAD: Qur'an surah 90, The City

AL BAQARAH: Qur'an surah 2, The Heifer

AL FATH: Qur'an surah 28, The Victory

AL FATIHAH: Qur'an surah 1, The Opening

AL HADID: Qur'an surah 57, Iron

AL HAJJ: Qur'an surah 22, The Pilgrimage

AL HAQQAH: Qur'an surah 69, The Sure Reality

AL HIJR: Qur'an surah 15, The Rocky Tract

AL HUJURAT: Qur'an surah 49, The Chambers

AL HUMAZAH: Qur'an surah 104, The Slanderer

AL INSAN: Qur'an surah 76, The Man

AL KAHF: Qur'an surah 18, The Cave

AL MA'ARIJ: Qur'an surah 70, The Ways of Ascent

AL MA'IDAH: Qur'an surah 5, The Repast

AL MA'UN: Qur'an surah 107, The Small Kindness

AL MU'MINUN: Qur'an surah 23, The Believers

AL MUDDATHTHIR: Qur'an surah 74, The Cloaked Ones

AL MULK: Qur'an surah 67, The Dominion

AL MUMTAHINAH: Qur'an surah 60, That which Examines

AL MUNAFIQUN: Qur'an surah 63, The Hypocrites

AL MUTAFFIFIN: Qur'an surah 83, The Defrauding

AL NAHL: Qur'an surah 16, The Bees

AL NAML: Qur'an surah 27, The Ant

AL NAS: Qur'an surah 114, Mankind

AL NISA': Qur'an surah 4, The Woman

AL NUR: Qur'an surah 24, The Light

AL QASAS: Qur'an surah 28, The Narrations

AL RA'D: Qur'an surah 13, The Thunder

AL SAFF: Qur'an surah 61, The Battle Array

AL SAFFAT: Qur'an surah 37, The Ranks

AL SHU'ARA: Qur'an surah 26, The Poets

AL SHURA: Qur'an surah 42, Consultation

AL TAGHABUN: Qur'an surah 64, The Mutual Loss and Gain

AL TAWBAH: Qur'an surah 9, The Repentance

AL ZUMAR: Qur'an surah 39, Crowds

Alagaddupama Sutta, MN 22, The Simile of the Snake

Al-Bayan wa al-Tabyin, Abu 'Uthman 'Amr b. Bahr Al-Jahiz, Eloquence and Demonstration, Tarif Khalidi version

Amos, KJV, Old Testament, Minor Prophets, 19 copies found among Dead Sea Scrolls

Anenjasappaya Sutta: MN 106, The Way to the Imperturbable

Antiquities of the Jews: Josephus, William Whiston version

Anuruddha Sutta: MN 127

Apollonius of Tyana: Philostratus, biography in 8 books, Christopher Jones version

Apollonius of Tyana letters: Christopher Jones translation, Greek Neo-Pythagorean philosopher who lived in the first century CE, according to Philostratus, he lived from 3 BCE to 97 CE.

Ariyapariyesana Sutta: MN 26, The Noble Search

Barnabas: early Christian, J.B. Lightfoot version

Bhaddekaratta Sutta: MN 131, A Single Excellent Night

Bhagavad Gita: Juan Mascaro version, Hindu classic

Bhikkhusamyutta: SN 21, Connected Discourses with Bhikkhus

Bojjhangasamyutta: SN 46, Connected Discourses on the Factory of Enlightenment

Brahmanasamyutta: SN 7, Connected Discourses with Brahmins

Canki Sutta: MN 95

Chandogya Upanishad: Uprising of the Sacred Song, Juan Mascaro version

Cittasamyutta: SN 41, With Citta

Corpus Hermeticum: Clement Salaman, Dorine van Oyen, William Wharton version, Alexandrian text second century CE

Culakammavibhanga Sutta: MN 135, A Shorter Exposition of Action

Culasaropama Sutta: MN 30, The Shorter Discourse on the Simile of Hardwood

Culasaccaka Sutta: MN 35, The Shorter Discourse to Saccaka

Culasunnata Sutta: MN 121, The Shorter Discourse on Voidness

Daniel: KJV, Old Testament, 8 copies found among Dead Sea Scrolls

Dead Sea Scrolls 4Q171, Commentary on Psalms

Dead Sea Scrolls 4Q424, A Collection of Proverbs

Dead Sea Scrolls 4Q473, The Two Ways

Dead Sea Scrolls 4Q525, The Blessings of the Wise

Dead Sea Scrolls Community Rule 1QS, Charter of a Jewish Sectarian Association

Dead Sea Scrolls Damascus Document, Zadokite Fragments, Geniza A+B being a tenth century Medieval copy, combined with 4Q266-272 Dead Sea Scroll fragments

Dead Sea Scrolls War Scroll 1QM, 1Q33

Deuteronomy, KJV, Old Testament, 33 copies found among Dead Sea Scrolls

Devaputtasamyutta: SN 2, Connected Discourses with Young Devas

Devatasamyutta: SN 1, Connected Discourses with Devatas

Dhammadayada Sutta: MN 3, Heirs in Dharma

Dhammapada: Khuddaka Nikaya, Juan Mascaro version

Dialogue of the Saviour: early Christian text, NHL 3.5, Emmel version

Didache, early Christian text, Kirsopp Lake version

Dvedhavitakka Sutta: MN 19, Two Kinds of Thought

Exodus: KJV, Old Testament, 18 copies found among Dead Sea Scrolls

Ezekiel: KJV, Old Testament, 6 copies found among Dead Sea Scrolls

FATIR: Qur'an surah 35, The Originator of Creation

FUSSILAT: Qur'an surah 41, Expounded

Galatians: KJV, New Testament

Gamanisamyutta: SN 42, Connected Discourses with Headmen

Ganaka Moggallana Sutta: MN 107

Genesis: KJV, Old Testament, 20 copies found among Dead Sea Scrolls

GHAFIR: Qur'an surah 40, Forgiver

Habakkuk: KJV, Old Testament, Minor Prophets, 10 copies found among Dead Sea Scrolls

HUD: Qur'an surah 11, The Prophet Hud

Hymn to Zeus: attributed to Cleanthes, Stoic, M.A.C. Ellery version

Iddhipadasamyutta: SN 51, Connected Discourses on the Bases for Spiritual Power

Isaiah: KJV, Old Testament, latest parts added first century CE, 21 copies found among Dead Sea Scrolls

James: KJV, New Testament

Jeremiah: KJV, Old Testament, 6 copies found among Dead Sea Scrolls

Job: KJV, Old Testament, 4 copies found among Dead Sea Scrolls

John: KJV, New Testament

Jubilees: Divisions of Time, 16 copies found among Dead Sea Scrolls, O.S. Wintermute version

Judges, KJV, Old Testament, 3 copies found among Dead Sea Scrolls

Kakacupama Sutta: MN 21, The Simile of the Saw

Kandaraka Sutta: MN 51

Katha Upanishad: Death as Teacher, Juan Mascaro version

Kena Upanishad: By Whom, Juan Mascaro version

Khandhasamyutta: SN 22, Connected Discourses on the Aggregates

Kitab al-Zuhd: Abu 'Abdallah Ahmad b. Muhammad al-Shaybani Ibn Hanbal, Pertaining to Piety, Tarif Khalidi version

Kitab al-Zuhd wa al-Raqa'iq: 'Abdallah al-Marwazi Ibn al-Mubarak, Pertaining to Piety and Softening of Hearts, Tarif Khalidi version

Kosalasamyutta: SN 3, Connected Discourses with Kosalan

Lamentations: KJV, Old Testament, 4 copies found among Dead Sea Scrolls

Leviticus, KJV, Old Testament, 16 copies found among Dead Sea Scrolls

Lotus Sutra: Burton Watson version, Sadharmapunparika Sutra, a Mahayana text

Luke: KJV, New Testament

LUQMAN: Qur'an surah 31, Wisdom

Maggasamyutta: SN 45, Connected Discourses on the Path

Maha-Assapura Sutta: MN 39, The Greater Discourse at Assapura

Mahadukkhakklandha Sutta: MN 13, The Greater Discourse on the Mass of Suffering

Mahagopalaka Sutta: MN 33, The Greater Discourse on the Cowherd

Mahapadana Sutta: DN 14, The Greater Discourse on the Lineage

Mahasunnata Sutta: MN 122, The Greater Discourse on Voidness

Mahavacchagotta Sutta: MN 73, The Greater Discourse to Vacchagatta

Mahavagga: Vinaya Pitaka, Kucchivikara-vatthu and Thanissaro Bhikkhu version

Maitri Upanishad: school of Krishna, Juan Mascaro version

Marasamyutta: MN 43, The greater Series of Questions and Answers

Mark: KJV, New Testament

MARYAM: Qur'an surah 19, Mary, the Mother of Jesus

Matthew: KJV, New Testament, the only known ancient document to contain the Sermon on the Mount

Metta Sutta: Karaniya Metta Sutta, The Discourse on Loving Kindness, Sutta Nipata 8, Khuddaka Nikaya, F.L. Woodward version

MUHAMMAD: Qur'an surah 47, Muhammad, The Prophet

Mundaka Upanishad: Shaven Head, Juan Mascaro version

Numbers: KJV, Old Testament, Benidbar (Desert), 11 copies found among Dead Sea Scrolls

Odyssey, Homer, ancient Greek poet, Samuel Butler version

Odes of Solomon: second century CE, used in Pistis Sophia, J.H Charlesworth version

Pistis Sophia: The Faith of Wisdom, important early Gnostic Christian text, J.J. Hurtak and Desiree Hurtak version

Proverbs: KJV, Old Testament, 2 copies found among Dead Sea Scrolls

Psalms: KJV, Old Testament, 37 copies found among Dead Sea Scrolls, used in Pistis Sophia

Psalms 154: found among Dead Sea Scrolls as text 11QPs 154, J.H. Charlesworth version

Psalms of Solomon: Jewish text from just before the dawn of Christianity, R.B. Wright version

Pseudo-Phocylides: Jewish text, attributed to Ionic poet, just before the dawn of Christianity, P.W. van der Horst version

QAF: Qur'an surah 50, The Matter has been Decreed

Ratthapala Sutta: MN 82

Revelation: KJV, New Testament

Romans: KJV, New Testament

Saccasamyutta: SN 56, Connected Discourses on the Truth

Sakkasamyutta: SN 11, Connected Discourses with Sakka

Salayatanasamyutta: SN 35, Connected Discourses on the Six Sense Bases

Sallekha Sutta: MN 8, Effacement

Samanamandika Sutta: MN 78

Satipatthana Sutta: MN 10, The Foundations of Mindfulness

Satipatthanasamyutta: SN 47, Connected Discourses on the Establishments of Mindfulness

Shepherd of Hermas Mandate: early Christian text, J.B. Lightfoot version

Shepherd of Hermas Parable: early Christian text, J.B. Lightfoot version

Sirach: KJV, Apocrypha, Dead Sea Scroll fragments, Ecclesiasticus, Jesus son of Sirach, Jewish text adopted by Christians

Sotapattisamyutta: SN 55, Connected Discourses on Stream-Entry

Spiritual Canticle: St. John of the Cross, Doctor of the Church, sixteenth century Christian mystic, Kicran Kavanaugh, Otilio Rodriguez version

Svetasvatara Upanishad: White Mule, Juan Mascaro version

TA HA: Qur'an surah 20, O Man!

Talmud: Berakoth: Seder Zera'im, Maurice Simon version

Talmud: Sotah: Seder Nashim, A. Cohen version

Tao Te Ching: Lao Tzu, primary text of Taoism, Gia-Fu Feng and Jane English version

Tathagata-garbha Sutra: Buddhabhadra, William Grosnick version

Tevijja Sutta: DN 13, The Way to Brahma [God]

Tevijjavacchagotta Sutta: MN 71, To Vacchagotta on the Threefold True Knowledge

Thomas: NHL 2.2, Lambdin version

Tobit: KJV, Apocrypha, 5 copies found among Dead Sea Scrolls

Udanavarga: Khuddaka Nukaya, Sara Boin-Webb version

Upakkilesa Sutta: MN 128, Imperfections

Vanapattha Sutta: MN 17, Jungle Thickets

Vangisasamyutta: SN 8, Connected Discourses on Vangisa

Vatthupama Sutta: MN 7, The Simile of the Cloth

Vitakkasanthana Sutta: MN 20, The Removal of Distracting Thoughts

Wars of the Jews: Josephus, William Whiston version

Wisdom of Solomon: KJV, Apocrypha, Jewish text adopted by Christians

YA SIN: Qur'an surah 36, O Leader of Man!

Yakkhasamyutta: SN 10, Connected Discourses with Yakkhas

YUNUS: Qur'an surah 10, Jonah

Zephaniah: KJV, Old Testament, Minor Prophets, 10 copies found among Dead Sea Scrolls

Print Index

Buddhist words:

arahant, mystic, liberated, accomplished

bhikkhu, disciple, Buddhist monk

brahma, god, deity (Hindu creator god)

brahmin, brahmana, saint, class of religious people

buddha, enlightened, awakened

dhamma, dharma, truth, law, states, factors, mind-objects, qualities, teachings

jhana, meditative state accomplished, absorption into an altered sense of reality

karma, kamma, action, justice. A related Pali word, kama, means the pleasures and desires associated with the senses. The Buddha's great insight, in short is, "no kama, no kamma".

metta, loving-kindness, similar to the Greek word agape

nirvana, nibbana, extinguished, final deliverance, freedom

samatha, samma, serenity, peacefulness, settlement, stilling. The related word in Pali, samma, means to fully and completely be right. The Noble Eightfold Path involves getting eight aspects of one's self in a state of samma.

sutra, sutta, thread

Hebrew words

The words are written the way they are to note that Hebrew has only consonant letters, which are represented capitalized, while the vowel sounds are accent marks, which are represent lower cased.

KaDoWSH: holy, set apart, distinct, one of a kind, precious

NeSHaMaH: warmth, heart, shared nature with God

TaMiYM: perfect, having integrity, being complete, whole, entire, without any loss, healthy

YeSHaH: salvation, as a proper name this is translated as Joshua from the Hebrew, the Greek LXX replacement for this name is translated into English as Jesus. This was a key word searched for in the scriptures by early Christians who were convinced that Jesus could be better understood by locating and interpreting these references (Acts 17.11).

ZaDoK: alms, acts of righteousness, the key term for the sacred group of revisionist Jews as described in the Damascus Document of the Dead Sea Scrolls.

Kabbalah Terms:

Jewish Kabbalah is legended to have begun in the first century CE, its insights hidden away and preserved and rediscovered in the Middle Ages. Part of its tradition is the relationship between key Hebrew words that are found in the scriptures.

BiYNaH: instinct, intuition, insight, vision, dream

CHeSeD: compassion, mercy, empathy, love, heart, similar to the Greek word agape

CHoKMaH: skill, accomplishment, learned realization, expertise

DaTH: decree, commandment, Law

GeBuWRaH: physical strength, force, energy

YeSoWD: presence, building, collected treasures, outward religion

173

Thomas Ragland is a native of Tennessee in the United States of America. Raised Southern Baptist Christian, his exploration of interfaith studies is seen through the lens of how the ideas relate back to the teachings of Jesus.

tomragland@excite.com

Also by Thomas Ragland:

The Noble Eightfold Path of Christ: Jesus Teaches the Dharma of Buddhism

2003

A survey of the teachings of Buddha on the Noble Eightfold Path and how the teachings of Jesus express the same timeless truths.

Paperback: ISBN-10: 1-4120-0013-0; ISBN-13: 978-1-4120-0013-0

Kindle: ASIN: B0027G6XT2

Nook: ISBN-13: 9781412210300

Buddha Turns the Kabbalah Wheel: Jewish Buddhist Resonance from a Christian Gnostic Perspective

2005

A study of Jewish Kabbalah and how the Buddhist Noble Eightfold Path and Three Gems harmonize as overlaying truths.

Paperback: ISBN-10: 1-4120-6461-9; ISBN-13: 978-1-4120-6461-3

Kindle: ASIN: B000QEC8FK

Nook: ISBN-13: 9781412238229

Jesus Gnosis Story of Simon by Philip

2009

A fictional story based on the people in the gospel stories, focused upon Simon Peter and Mary Magdalene, based on the legend that the early Christians fled to Pella to avoid the war in Jerusalem.

Paperback: ISBN-10: 1-4269-1365-6; ISBN-13: 978-1-4269-1365-5

Kindle: ASIN: B00332EW9W

Nook: BN ID: 2940016320212

www.ingramcontent.com/pod-product-compliance
Lightning Source LLC
Chambersburg PA
CBHW022131080426
42734CB00006B/307